ON OUR ORIGINS

Jen,
Nothing is impossible
with God! Luke 1:37

Pastor DC

ON OUR ORIGINS

DANIEL J. LEPLEY

WestBow
PRESS
A DIVISION OF THOMAS NELSON

WestBow Press books may be ordered through booksellers or by contacting:

WestBow Press
A Division of Thomas Nelson
1663 Liberty Drive
Bloomington, IN 47403
www.westbowpress.com
1-(866) 928-1240

ISBN: 978-1-4497-9531-3 (e)
ISBN: 978-1-4497-9530-6 (sc)
ISBN: 978-1-4497-9532-0 (hc)

Library of Congress Control Number: 2013909247

Printed in the United States of America.

WestBow Press rev. date: 5/31/2013

To my wife and children,
our family at Redeemer,
and all who seek Truth.

TABLE OF CONTENTS

BEFORE WE BEGIN

In the 1830s, an unknown British naturalist set sail on a journey that became a lifelong quest to discover the origins of the human race. He was far from the first person to ponder the beginnings of humanity and is certainly not the last to do so. What has made his journey remarkable is the effect his conclusions have had on how the human race has come to understand its origins.

In the introduction of his book, *On the Origin of Species*, Charles Darwin stated his conviction that the human intellect finally could grasp how life came to its present state. Equipped with his impressions of the natural order and loads of evidence to defend his radical new theory, Darwin optimistically stated, "These facts seemed to throw some light on the origin of species—that mystery of mysteries, as it has been called by one of our greatest philosophers. On my return home, it occurred to me, in 1837, that something might perhaps be made out on this question by patiently accumulating and reflecting on all sorts of facts which could possibly have any bearing on it."[1]

Not only has something been "made out" of his theory, but his ideas have completely rewritten humanity's understanding of life. His ideas proved so influential that they have now become the foundation of the life sciences.

Darwin recognized the potential of his theories to revolutionize how we understand our origins and clairvoyantly predicted that his theory would become the basis of many fields of study: "In the distant future I see open fields for far more important researches. Psychology will be based on a new foundation, that of the necessary acquirement of each mental power and capacity by gradation. Light will be thrown on the origin of man and his history."[2]

Darwin's prediction has proven true. His evolutionary model now serves as the foundation of sciences as diverse as biology, geology, psychology, and sociology. His theories have had such far-reaching implications that they now form the framework within which most people today—even most people of faith—try to understand themselves and where they've come from. His ideology has become ingrained in our collective consciousness.

Reflecting on Darwin's impact on both culture and the sciences, we would be mistaken to view Darwin as a genius who arrived at his conclusions in a vacuum. By the time of his rise to popularity in the nineteenth century, the world had already experienced many awakenings. The theory of evolution, birthed in the mind of Darwin, simply grew out of humanity's already changing understanding of the universe, life, and self. A culture dominated by the Christian church, with God at the center of humanity's understanding of existence, was found by many to no longer be acceptable.

By proposing a new explanation for humanity's origin and life based strictly upon natural knowledge, Darwin substituted a purely naturalistic view of humanity and life's origins. His view naturally grew out of his purely scientific mindset. Because God cannot be observed physically, all theories based upon a purely naturalistic scientific method will, by necessity, be godless or potentially anti-God.

Darwin's contribution to the sciences tipped the scales in favor of a much more naturalistic analysis of human origins. Before the rise of secularism (greatly accelerated in the sciences by Darwin's theory of natural selection and later by Einstein's theory of relativity), the church had been the largely undisputed arbiter of truth in the Christian West.[3] People had generally accepted the premise that God had revealed the true nature of existence and humanity's origin in the Scriptures.[4]

We now find ourselves living in a culture awash in the confluence of two strikingly different explanations of humanity's origins. Much of the current conflict and confusion about human origins likely stems from the different foundations upon which the institutions of religion and science are built. The faithful have traditionally viewed the *revealed* knowledge of God in the Scriptures[5] and the church as authoritative in matters of faith and life. In contrast, a scientific community, now secularized, proposes *natural* knowledge as the exclusive source of truth.

Before discussing the specifics of the secular and scriptural worldviews, it helps to acknowledge the basis of these differing explanations of humanity's origins. Do these divergent ways of looking at the world need to be mutually exclusive? Some have said yes; others have suggested no. Taking time to examine the interplay between these two methodologies is beneficial regardless of one's creed, because the examination provides the opportunity for informed reflection upon the mystery of mysteries in hopes of learning the most basic truth foundational to human existence.

THE SCRIPTURAL WORLDVIEW

The church, since the time of Christ, has been built upon the confession of Jesus Christ as Lord and Savior. This is heard clearly in an episode recorded by St. Matthew in the first gospel:

> Now when Jesus came into the district of Caesarea Philippi, he asked his disciples, "Who do people say that the Son of Man is?" And they said, "Some say John the Baptist, others say Elijah, and others Jeremiah or one of the prophets." He said to them, "But who do you say that I am?" Simon Peter replied, "You are the

Christ, the Son of the living God." And Jesus answered him, "Blessed are you, Simon Bar-Jonah! *For flesh and blood has not revealed this to you, but my Father who is in heaven.* And I tell you, you are Peter, and on this rock I will build my church. (Matthew 16:13–18a, emphasis added)

Here, Jesus explicitly stated that the revealed knowledge of God is essential for knowing the truth about God and the true nature of existence.

This revealed knowledge comes from a different source than scientific knowledge. It is based upon a supernatural knowledge given by God's Holy Spirit as revealed and preserved in the Scriptures. This revelation includes the overarching story of God's relationship with His creation, especially humanity, and provides Christians with a framework within which human reason operates. It is not contrary to reason but rather equips the human mind with faith to interpret existence from God's perspective instead of an exclusively anthropocentric (human centered) view of life.

St. John also recorded an episode in which Jesus explained to His disciples that He was the key to understanding the God of the Scriptures. Jesus said to Thomas, "I am the way, and the truth, and the life. No one comes to the Father except through me. If you had known me, you would have known my Father also. From now on you do know him and have seen him" (John 14:6-7). Here, Jesus asserted that because He is *the* way, truth, and life, the only path by which humanity can come to an accurate understanding of God (and consequently the true nature of reality) is to know Him.

According to the teaching of the apostles, the Bible began with God's creative work, is centered on Christ and will conclude at the consummation of all things. Throughout the course of His work, God promised to care for His people and all that He created by sending humanity a Savior. He and His love for humanity would not remain abstract, but He would reveal them clearly in the person of Jesus Christ. For Christians, everything comes together in Jesus of Nazareth, the historical person, because in Jesus, God made Himself known in ways that humanity can comprehend.

The traditional Christian worldview, which is based upon the revelation of God in the Scriptures, is therefore Christ-centered. It is based upon a revelation of God in the person of His Son, Jesus Christ. It is based on the belief that in the Bible, God reveals to humanity a reality deeper than what is apparent to the naked eye.

Suffice it to say that a Christ-centered worldview is not anti-science. Yes, the basis for a Christ-centered worldview is the *revealed* knowledge of God, who has manifested Himself in the Scriptures and in the person of His Son. God does not, however, give this revelation at the expense of reason or science. According to the Scriptures, revealed and natural knowledge are complementary parts of God's revelation to humanity.

There are parts of God's revelation that, since the time of the apostles, the church has labeled as "mystery," which means "beyond human comprehension."[6] Never in the Scriptures is the mystery of God invoked to deny the proper use of reason. The Scriptures instead simply acknowledge that certain things in life (including God) defy purely naturalistic human sensibilities.

We are and always will be limited in our understanding of what we can perceive through our five senses. The confines of the human mind also limit our depth of knowledge. A Christ-centered worldview equips Christians with the revealed knowledge of God—a scriptural big picture—within which they are free to explore and learn about the world.

THE CONFLICT BETWEEN CHURCH AND SCIENTIFIC COMMUNITIES IS BORN

Unfortunately, much hostility now exists between the church and many proponents of an exclusively secular scientific view of human origins. This is partly a result of past ecclesiastical practice. Historically, the church's hierarchy often resisted scientific theories on dogmatic grounds. This happened often before and during the Enlightenment, when many Protestant and Roman Catholic leaders used the Scriptures to deny emerging science. These misunderstandings from hundreds of years ago persist to this day.

The debate about the heliocentric (sun-centered) model of the solar system offered two high-profile instances of the church's unfortunate misuse of Scripture to deny science. Copernicus was among the first to suggest that the earth revolves around the sun. Upon hearing of this new thought, Martin Luther denounced his theory: "This would be as if somebody were riding on a cart or in a ship and imagined that he was standing still while the Earth and the trees were moving."[7]

Galileo was also persecuted for his insistence that the sun, not the earth, was the center of this corner of the universe. He was hauled before the Roman Catholic Inquisition twice to explain his theory. Although he wasn't executed or tortured by the Inquisition, he was ordered not to teach his heliocentric model of the solar system as fact; thus, his science was suppressed (even if not outright condemned).

Some Christians may invoke God, faith, or the Scriptures to deny the proper use of reason and science, but this causes more harm than good. The church's reluctance to investigate and then embrace science that has been demonstrated as fact has pitted religion against science and set up an inherent distrust of science and scientists that persists in some corners of the church to this day. It could also be argued that in much of the church, the pendulum has swung too far to the opposite extreme as some Christians embrace unproven scientific theories in an attempt to be culturally relevant. In either case, there is an often uneasy relationship between the church and the scientific community.

Learning from mistakes of the past, a Christ-centered worldview sees reason and science as gifts of God that, when properly used, unlock some of the mysteries of the natural realm, all to the glory of God and the benefit of faith. It is a blessing, not a curse, to grow in the understanding of the natural realm. Science is the tool best suited for this purpose, so long as scientific theory and implications are limited to the study of the physical realm.

THE SECULAR SCIENTIFIC WORLDVIEW

In contrast to the scriptural worldview, which is based upon the revealed knowledge of God in Jesus Christ, an exclusively scientific worldview is based upon natural knowledge. Scientific inquiry is limited to what can be observed physically. As such, science has no faculty for factoring into any explanation of existence the spiritual or divine.

This may frustrate many Christians who want to find evidence for their faith in science, looking for science to prove the existence of God. Pure observational science doesn't deal directly with questions of God or the spiritual realm, because empirical science is limited to what can be physically observed, replicated by experiment, and therefore proven. Secular science is at best Christ-less, because you can't put God in a test tube or see Him in a microscope or telescope.

Ever since Copernicus, Galileo, and Newton, there has been an uneasy tension between the church and the scientific community. Pure empirical science is built upon a belief that the only way human beings can learn is through their five senses. To be demonstrated, testable, and proven true, scientific inquiry must be limited to the physical realm.

Just as many church officials were guilty during the rise of science for standing in the way of scientific progress, many scientists now use purely naturalistic arguments to deny the spiritual realm. When science oversteps its bounds and begins to make assertions about the spiritual realm (or lack thereof) based upon what is observed in the physical realm, much confusion quickly follows.

Limited to natural knowledge, science can't deal directly with the spiritual.

For many, science (which even according to Darwin was originally intended to discover the laws impressed on matter by the Creator)[8] has become a method of and the reason for denying God. Over centuries of scientific inquiry, enough knowledge about the material realm has been stockpiled to lead many in the scientific community to conclude that the material realm is all that exists. Many have convinced themselves that there really isn't any need for God.

The reasoning that sometimes follows is that if we can imagine a universe where God isn't necessary, then God must not exist. With this mindset, the observer gets to set the parameters and determine all of the rules, so long as they are in accord with what is perceived of the natural order. Ever distancing itself from any notion of the divine, secular humanism has become an inherently self-centered view of life and the universe.

Humanity has had great success in figuring out *how* the physical realm currently operates. There has been so much advancement that entirely new fields of science—purely theoretical science— have been born in an attempt to answer the question *why*. What began as a godless attempt to explain *how* the universe works has evolved into a godless or even anti-God attempt to find the reason *why* everything exists.

This is where the current conflict between faith and science comes to a head. As soon as science moves from the realm of empirical, observational, testable (and therefore verifiable) study of the physical realm, it risks infringing upon the spiritual realm. Some scientists have boundless faith that there is no God. Others have boundless faith in God. Both secular and Christian scientists may be competent and intelligent enough to discover new and exciting aspects of the physical realm humans occupy, but their faith may very well lead them to entirely different conclusions regarding the implications of their discoveries.

The conflict between Christian and secular scientists continues in part because neither can prove the foundational origin theories of the other wrong based upon classical observational science. People simply can't send observers back in time to observe, sample, and prove exactly *how* all things came to be, let alone demonstrate empirically *why* they have assumed their present form. For this reason, there will most likely be an air of mystery about our origins until the end of time.

NE'ER THE TWAIN SHALL MEET?

There are few places one can go in this world where faith and science are not both present. These are two of the most significant pillars of society, right up there with the rule of law. They are even bigger than institutions, because both are part of the fabric of our culture and factor into every twenty-first-century human being's concept of origin and self.

There is tension between these two basic views of human origins for many reasons. They have mutually exclusive bases for their ideologies. The basis of one is a revealed knowledge of God in the Scriptures, while the other is only concerned with natural knowledge. This means they operate with vastly different approaches and means.

Both have also laid claim to the domain of ultimate truth. Both have provided people with much good and have also been used against humanity to accomplish much evil. But do discerning human beings who want to have the most holistic knowledge of the true nature of existence have to choose between faith and science?

Many on both sides of the debate insist that you can't have it both ways. I happen to believe that every human being, whether he or she is aware of it or not, doesn't exist without some measure of knowledge of the material and spiritual domain. We live in a physical realm and all have faith in something. The "something" that ultimately directs your choices in life, which is the reason for everything you hold to be true, is your god.[9]

We live in a culture that is very spiritual and yet secular and science-driven. If we are to come to a correct understanding of our realm, ourselves, and our God, it is essential for us to come to terms with our beginnings. The reason the study of beginnings has been one of the essential quests of humanity since the dawn of civilization is that where we've come from will inform us of who we are and where we are headed.

Every person—whether he or she is a person of faith or not—strives on a lifelong quest to figure out his or her identity. *Who am I?* We also strive to make an impact or a difference. *Who will I become?* Most people would like to make an impact that lasts longer than their time upon the earth. *How will I be remembered?* Keenly aware of our mortality, we also want to know what, if anything, lies before us when this life is over. *Where am I going?*

You will answer each of these questions for yourself. How you live will demonstrate how you answer these questions. This is true whether or not you understand how or why you've become who you are.

What is observed in science (natural knowledge) and what is perceived by faith (revealed knowledge) both form our decisions to the above questions. However, when we demonize faith or science, we are held back from achieving a full understanding of self, why we've done what we've done, and how we've become who we are.

Reason to Believe or Not to Believe

Since a creation story is the foundation of both the secular scientific and Christ-centered worldviews, we will examine the framework of both creation accounts in light of each other. The study of origins covers fields as diverse as astronomy, biology, cosmology, geology, mathematics, physics, psychology, sociology, theology, and others. Because such a wide range of fields and topics will be breached, exploration of the key components of origins theory will follow the order of creation described by Moses. By drawing from divergent fields and the work of many who *don't* agree on much of anything regarding the origins of the universe and humanity, those of a scientific and/or a Christ-centered mindset will grow in their understanding of many issues at the heart of the debate about human origins.

Where you think you've come from will determine who you are and your view of your future (or lack thereof). In other words, how you answer the questions about your origin will provide the default answer to every question about your identity, purpose, and future. This is why origins theory is so important. Your foundational view of reality is the basis of every answer to every question about your identity.

Adrift in a flood of competing theories and so-called proof of where humanity has come from, many have drowned in disillusionment with science or faith. Is faith the enemy of science, as some have suggested?[10] Is secularism the greatest current threat to personal faith and the cultural relevance of the church? Until becoming acquainted with the basis of both worldviews, no one can have a fully informed answer to such questions.

Before Darwin, Christianity was the predominant culture of Western Civilization. Martin Rees has recently noted that science has now become the global culture.[11] As we recognize the past and look forward to the future, it is important to be conversant from both vantage points. This study will help people make more informed decisions regarding the most important questions in this life. Even if the reader rejects what is proposed, at least he or she will have a better understanding of what he or she is rejecting and potential implications for his or her future.

NEW BEGINNINGS

When Charles Darwin published his book *The Origin of Species*, the world was ripe for a new explanation of life's beginnings. A new worldview was in order, based solely upon observational science and the natural order of things. The old order, with God and the church at the helm, seemed to keep humanity from achieving its full potential. Drawing heavily upon rationalism and an increasingly naturalistic view of the world, humanity grew by leaps and bounds in its understanding of self and the world. Unbridled optimism led to faith in the human intellect's ability to discover the true nature of existence. The world was primed for a purely naturalistic, godless explanation of all things.

Mr. Darwin sought to shed light on the "mystery of mysteries" by explaining how natural processes could account for the variety of creatures and geological formations he observed in his travels aboard the *H.M.S. Beagle* and in his native Great Britain. Everywhere he traveled, there were peculiarities about living things that didn't reconcile with his notions of how the world should operate, had all living creatures been formed by a divine being. In his opinion, "independent acts of creation" didn't adequately account for the arrangement and distribution of creatures in the wild. He observed too many oddities for which his theology had no adequate explanation. He couldn't reconcile his observations and the conclusions other naturalists drew from observational science with the teachings of Christian scientists of his time: "Authors of highest eminence seem to be fully satisfied with the view that each species has been independently created. To my mind it accords better with what we know of the laws impressed on matter by the Creator, that the production and extinction of the past and present inhabitants of the world should have been due to secondary causes."[12] Darwin used a multitude of illustrations to prove his point, drawing from the forces he observed at work in the world.

One example was bats, which were the only mammals Darwin observed inhabiting many remote islands in the vast oceans. In his travels, he noticed that there were many species of bats living on isolated islands (some hundreds of miles from the nearest land mass) scattered all over the southern hemisphere. On these islands, no native land mammals could be found. Unable to figure out why "the supposed creative force" would have decided to place flying mammals on these islands but not land mammals, he suggested that there was no such creative force at work there. Instead, he believed that these bats had managed to fly hundreds of miles oversea and evolve into species unique to each place.[13]

Darwin also noted the presence of body parts that have no apparent current use. Two examples within the human body that Darwin singled out as vestiges of ancient evolutionary ancestors were nipples on males[14] and the tailbone.[15] Both of these parts of the human body were, in his opinion, worthless and remainders of organs that had become obsolete due to the work of natural selection. These clues led him to the conclusion that natural selection, not "the ordinary doctrine of creation," was the method by which all organisms have come to their present form.[16] Darwin knew it would take millions of years for this to happen. Drawing from the work of Charles Lyell and others, he looked to the geological record, entombed in layers of stone, to find evidence of the length of time it would have taken for natural selection to produce multitudes of life forms.[17]

In the conclusion of his masterful work, Darwin explicitly connected his theories to the work begun by Sir Isaac Newton, who may be considered the father of observational science: "There is grandeur in this view of life, with its several powers, having been originally breathed into a few forms or into one; and that, whilst this planet has gone cycling on according to the fixed law of gravity, from so simple a beginning endless forms most beautiful and most wonderful have been, and are being, evolved."[18] Although Darwin acknowledged the necessity of some pre-existing power in order to "breathe life" into the first life form,[19] his successors would base the case for a godless world upon his groundbreaking theories.

A trained naturalist with a sharp eye, Darwin made a convincing case that natural selection, not "special acts of creation,"[20] tweaked the organization of living beings into more and more complex life forms that eventually evolved into the human race. During the nineteenth century, biologists, anthropologists, and archeologists began to search for the missing links in humanity's evolutionary family tree. They continued their search and refined Darwin's theories into the next century. But another unforeseen advancement in science was coming that would turn much of the scientific community's attention up to the heavens in the search for the raw building blocks of life.

If Darwin succeeded in leading the nineteenth-century quest for answers to life's origin in fossils and rocks, Einstein and others turned the gaze of twentieth-century scientists to the stars in their quest to assemble the puzzle of human origins. Just as the ancients looked to the stars in their search for the meaning of their existence, modern science would do the same, albeit in a much more technologically advanced way. With a godless explanation for how life evolved in one hand, humanity's attention turned to looking for a godless source of matter for the other.

FROM THE BIOLOGICAL TO THE COSMOLOGICAL

Early in the twentieth century, Albert Einstein revolutionized the way scientists understood the universe with his twin theories of general and special relativity. Amongst other things, the theory of relativity set forth paradigms that radically altered how people view the operation of the universe from the infinitesimally small to the infinitely grand scale. According to relativity, everything in the universe is not static, as the ancients believed. Indeed, matter (the stuff and fluff of all creation), energy, time, space, and the laws that govern the relationship between these forces are no longer thought of independently, because they have been demonstrated to be in flux with each other.

In the simplest layperson's terms, Einstein, for the first time in human history, demonstrated that energy can be converted into matter and that matter can be converted into energy. The world-famous equation associated with this theory is $E=mc^2$. This beautifully simple equation demonstrates the equivalency of energy and mass.[21]

Before relativity, matter was viewed as eternal and unchangeable, with energy being one of the many forces that worked on matter. But Einstein predicted, and experiment has proven, that matter can be converted into energy. We literally see evidence of his theory at work every day the sun rises, shining bright with the energy produced by atoms of hydrogen fusing into helium, thereby releasing the energy that powers the sun.

Previously, people assumed that matter was comprised of stuff, not of energy. But Einstein showed that in essence, photons (energy) are possibly the building blocks of all matter. Matter was viewed as eternal. Now, matter and energy became viewed as relative.

In the wake of Einstein, no longer does the pavement one walks on seem to be, well, so concrete. From our perspective, it appears to be very hard—a nearly impenetrable barrier between us and the earth beneath. But if we were to break it down into its most basic parts—from molecules to atoms to subatomic protons, neutrons, and electrons and from there to sub-subatomic quarks, photons, etc., we would be left with an immense amount of relatively massless energy. This is because raw energy seems to be what physical stuff is composed of.

In light of the theory of relativity, the big bang theory was conceived as a purely naturalistic beginning of the universe. This new theory offered a purely naturalistic answer to the question of whom or what is the source of all that exists. All living organisms are composed of matter and need energy to live. Stars provide both. Could the universe all by itself and the stars that light the night sky be the sources of life?

Stephen Hawking describes the effects of relativity on humanity's conception of how the universe may have begun: "In the following decades, this new understanding of space and time was to revolutionize our view of the universe. The old idea of an essentially unchanging universe that could have existed, and could continue to exist, forever was replaced by the notion of a dynamic, expanding universe that seemed to have begun a finite time ago, and that might end at a finite time in the future."[22]

The theory of relativity has provided a basis for a belief in a beginning—a moment of creation, if you will. It also contained new possibilities for a framework within which humanity could find its place in the cosmos apart from a Creator God.

Scientists have since looked intently to the heavens in order to find evidence of the pressure cooker of a young, rapidly expanding universe that would be verification of the big bang. All the while assembling a purely naturalistic model of a "creative moment" capable of producing an abundance of light elements (hydrogen, helium, and lithium).[23] These elements are still observed as the bulk of the nuclear fuel for fusion reactions occurring in stars throughout the known universe.

Here are some of the big discoveries that have fueled the growing acceptance of the big bang theory as a reasonable explanation of the universe's origin:

- Early in his career as an astronomer, Edwin Hubble was the first person to observe objects outside of our universe. He then demonstrated that these objects were moving away from earth, suggesting that the universe is expanding.

- Two Americans, Arno Penzias and Robert Wilson, accidentally discovered cosmic background radiation (CBR). First thought to be excess noise they picked up with their radio telescope, this was evidence consistent with what scientists hoped to hear as the echo of the big bang.[24]

- Following the initial discovery of CBR, further observations were made using earth-based and satellite-based imaging equipment to map this radiation. What was found verified what astronomers predicted. It looks like the ancient universe was a very "hot" place, dense with energy and ripe for the creation of the forces and matter of the physical realm.[25]

- The early universe wasn't entirely uniform, which is a good thing if you are a fan of the big bang, because the "wrinkles" of the early universe allowed for mass to settle into "lumps" that would become the birthing grounds of entire galaxies full of stars.[26]

- Theoretical physicists have shown the mathematical possibilities of matter and antimatter that can apparently spring in and out of existence.[27]

- The existence of matter and antimatter, which spontaneously appears and disappears, has opened the door to a belief in the universe being created from literally nothing.[28]

Belief in the big bang has accelerated general acceptance of a godless explanation of human origins. Entire fields of research and multibillion dollar efforts have been launched to prove this theory true. Thousands of scientists regularly make new discoveries that contribute fresh insights fueling the overwhelming discussion of the question, "Where did we come from?"

Now equipped with telescopes able to peer all the way back to the brink of the beginning of time, some scientists are cautiously optimistic that we are very close to a satisfactory explanation of how life came to into existence without needing to invoke God. Some seem intent to conclude that everything was produced from literally nothing. It is now accepted as popular fact that the earth is the daughter of a solar system, herself the daughter of a galaxy that is just a tiny fraction of the known universe that leapt into existence 13.7 billion years ago.[29]

These findings, according to leading cosmologist Lawrence Krauss, prove that all life on earth has descended from the stars: "One of the most poetic facts I know about the universe is that essentially every atom in your body was once inside a star that exploded. Moreover, the atoms in your left hand probably came from a different star than did those in your right. We are all, literally, star children, and our bodies made of star dust."[30] He continues, "Over the course of the history of our galaxy, about 200 million stars have exploded. These myriad stars sacrificed themselves, if you wish, so that one day you could be born. I suppose that qualifies them as much as anything else for the role of saviors."[31] The implication raised by many secular researchers is that humanity finally has enough scientific evidence to do away with God.

Humanity was set on a trajectory toward a godless explanation of origins by the mid-nineteenth century, if not sooner. Darwin's proposed framework of purely natural causes being the reason behind the diversity of life took hold of the collective imagination of scientists around the globe. Couple Darwin's purely naturalistic bent with Einstein's theory regarding the substance of life, add a theoretical cosmological perspective, and you have the basis of an entirely new, purely naturalistic and scientific foundation for explaining the origin of the universe, life, and humanity. Darwin opened the door to this ideology, and nearly all of science has rushed through. To prove his case, evidence to support his view is sought by secular scientists from the outer reaches of space to the deepest parts of the oceans to the innermost bowels of the earth.

This insatiable quest for knowledge, apart from the Creator God whom Darwin acknowledged as the initial giver of life, brought open conflict between the church and the scientific community to a boiling point. Current debates over whether or not God is a necessary part of the picture of the universe is the continuation of a conflict that began at the time of Copernicus and Galileo. If there is enough evidence to do away with God and this battle has raged for hundreds of years, why does it still persist?

Is "Who's Right, and Who's Wrong?" the Right Question to Ask?

Even though a true knowledge of ultimate reality is at stake, the hardcore proponents of the scientific and religious communities seem content, in the debate about origins, to talk past each other. In an increasingly polarized society, it seems easier for leaders of the religious and scientific communities to build their cases upon the assumption that the other is wrong on all counts. Just as political parties now have a tendency to lean on their bases to win elections (by placating their constituencies instead of honestly compromising to find a true middle way), both sides of the God-and-science debate often fail to truly engage each other. This forces people into a false dichotomy—an unreasonable and (as we will learn) unfortunate choice between God and science.

Whether one chooses to believe in or deny faith or science, it is wise to first know what you are agreeing with or denying. Every person listens to both scientific and religious authorities to a greater or lesser degree. Some have well-reasoned positions, but most have simply accepted what they've been told is true.

To help interested parties come to a more accurate understanding of the dynamics of this ongoing discussion regarding faith and science, we will explore a traditional rendering of the Genesis story of creation in light of current scientific observations. Science has its place in discovering how the natural world operates. Theology, not so concerned with answering the question of *how,* is better suited to help humanity see itself within the story of God's activity by proposing answers to the question, "Why do all things exist?"

When either side oversteps its bounds and ventures recklessly into the field of the other, damage is done to the innocent. The fact is that we live in a physical world, but human beings are not merely physical creatures. We have intellect, will, the ability to decide, emotion, social lives, and spiritual natures. It seems there is a part of every human that longs for more than just what meets the eye—a deeper meaning that makes life make sense. If this were not true, how else would you account for all of the religions and places of worship around the world?

Everyone has faith in something—a god she or he worships or looks to for the answer to life's most profound questions. From a theological perspective, the question is not whether or not someone believes in God. The real question is, "Which god do you worship as the true God?"

Society depends on science, which has brought many advancements and much good to humanity. Many diseases have been cured, barriers between people are being torn down, and the world experiences new levels of security and prosperity through the advancement of science and its application to daily life. In light of all the good science does society, many a person of faith is left wondering, *How can science, which affords so much good, be so dangerous—or even evil—according to many church authorities?*

Society also depends on people being good citizens and putting others first. The church has much to offer the world in her attempts to rectify many of the world's ills. As her adherents grow in their knowledge of and relationship with their God, they become positive forces in the world. Few institutions could hold a candle to the church in her ability to give people a sense of meaning, hope for the future, and good reason to be positive influences. Evidence of the goodwill Christians have shown humanity can be seen in the number of American hospitals that were started by churches. But many question how people can have faith in an institution in which many stubbornly hold on to outdated and irrelevant truths that are widely condemned by the scientific community as contrary to fact.

It seems that the human race is no closer to agreement about common origins in the twenty-first century than ever. This is despite thousands of years' worth of speculation on the question, "Where did everything come from?" We may actually be much further separated from each other due to dramatically different understandings built upon mutually exclusive foundations of thought. This deadlock flows from the false dichotomy that pits science against God.

In humanity's quest to understand its place in the cosmos, one explanation that has not changed since the dawn of civilization is the Genesis account of creation. Almost every other religious account for human beginnings has been jettisoned by most of its adherents, but the biblical model still stands. Why? Could there be something about this particular story that can't be disproven—that could have some clues to the "mystery of mysteries"?

IN THE BEGINNING, GOD …

The Genesis account was recorded 3,500 years ago by a cosmopolitan leader whose writings are the foundational Scriptures of Judaism and Christianity. Even though Moses was born to Hebrew slaves, he was raised as the adopted son of an Egyptian princess and afforded every advantage of Egyptian nobility. Later in life, he despised the wealth and influence that came with his adoption and found his faith and his place within the story of Israel, God's chosen people. After experiencing a midlife crisis and struggling to find his own place in a conflicted world, Moses spent forty years in the wilderness as a reclusive shepherd. This hiatus gave him much time to think things through and discuss his ideas with the few travelers and traders with whom he crossed paths.

Given Moses' education and life experiences, one could expect that his explanation of the creation of all things would have relied heavily upon Egyptian and Babylonian accounts. Well-trained, with a diverse cultural, religious, and educational background, when he became the leader of the Hebrew people, he would have been in a perfect position to cook up a hybrid view of the Egyptian and Babylonian creation stories and peddle this tale as an inspired version. He could have easily chosen to blend the two predominant views of creation at his time, showing deference to the two great nations on either side of the land of Israel.

But in the first few chapters of Genesis, the most significant shared themes of the creation accounts from Israel's influential neighbors aren't present. As a matter of fact, Moses' account stands in stark contrast to both the Egyptian and Babylonian creation myths. The other creation accounts involved multiple deities; Moses only named one. Instead of creation springing from conflict, there is peaceful harmony and order in Genesis 1–2. Whereas Egypt and Babylon claimed that earth was a reforming of what had existed before, there was no preexisting matter in Moses' account—only absolute nothingness apart from God. Nor did the Genesis story give any deference to the sun or a sun god. Moses told an entirely different tale.

An Introduction to God—Elohim

The most important element of the Genesis account is its central character, God. He is the beginning of the story, because everything in the Genesis account (which, according to Moses, includes everything in the natural realm) originates with God. He existed before the universe. According to Moses' description, God formed everything by merely speaking it into existence. He is a being powerful enough to make things happen by the verbal expression of His will.

How does a human author go about trying to describe someone or something that surpasses the bounds of human reason and language? Moses' God is the eternal and all-powerful source of everything that exists. It would be a tall order to relate the indescribable in an intelligible way. So Moses began his story of creation by introducing a God who so surpassed anything in the universe that even His Name, Elohim (pronounced El-o-*heem*), confounds the normal grammatical operation of human language.

Moses was a well-educated and proficient writer, despite his apparent fear of public speaking and a possible speech impediment.

He would have certainly understood basic Hebrew grammar. For example, if Moses wanted to say that God made two distinct things in English, you would assume that he would have written a simple sentence that would look something like this: "God made the heavens and the earth" (a singular masculine noun followed by a verb with two direct objects joined by a conjunction). This very basic sentence makes sense, and most translations render the opening verse of the Bible similarly to this.

But in the opening words of the Hebrew Bible, Moses did something one wouldn't expect. Instead of using the singular Hebrew noun for *god* (transliterated *el*), Moses used the plural form of the word for *gods* (El-o-*heem*). A first glance at the noun tells you there is more than one god doing this creating, but the verb for *create* is a third-person singular verb. This means that the verb and noun are not in agreement, because *create* is singular, but *gods* is plural.

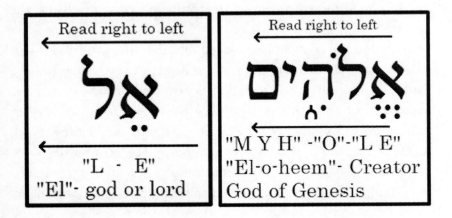

The opening words of Genesis, literally translated, are "In the beginning, Gods created the heavens and the earth." This begs the question, why the apparent contradiction in number? Instead of chiding Moses for his grammatical ineptitude or treating this sentence as a mistake, it makes more sense to believe that this was intentional. As a matter of fact, this tradition of referring to the Hebrew Creator God as *Elohim* is carried throughout the rest of the books of Moses and the Hebrew Scriptures.

The construction Moses employed is odd and confusing, because it doesn't make grammatical sense. You don't have to be an English or Hebrew major to see the apparent contradiction here. Even a four-year-old child knows that nouns and verbs must be in agreement. To say "the duck swims" is correct. To say "the ducks swim" is also correct. But to say "the ducks swims" is not proper grammar. It doesn't make sense, because the verb and the noun are not in agreement.

Was Moses simply trying to say that his God was above all others, or is this how the God of the Scriptures revealed Himself to Moses? Even though many gods were known and worshipped at the time of Moses, the Creator God is the only God ever referred to by Moses or other Old Testament authors as the singular God *Elohim*. There are many *els,* or gods, but only one true, singular God. Make no mistake—according to the Hebrew Scriptures, the one true God is Elohim.

There is a ton of meaning packed into that one little noun—an allusion that there is much more than meets the eye when talking about God Elohim, who created the earth and universe. By using the plural Elohim with the third-person singular form of the verb "create," Moses explicitly stated that his God, the Hebrew God, was far above and beyond any other god by His very nature.

Elohim's existence as the beginningless Creator in existence before the physical realm existed is more than we can fathom. By His very nature, He is supernatural. According to Moses, as the exclusive Creator of all things, Elohim is above all other gods. He is the source of all that exists.

Within this oneness of God, there is an implicit multiplicity. The plural construct of God's Name, Elohim, indicates that more than one person exists in this Creator God. In Genesis 1:2, Moses mentioned the Spirit of God. This Spirit is a distinct person from

Elohim yet still God. "Over the face of the deep the Spirit of Elohim was hovering" (Genesis 1:2b). Some may try to explain this away as a figurative reference to God's presence. But when taken as another person of the Godhead, we can begin to see that the best way to reconcile the grammatical inconsistency of the opening sentence is to acknowledge that there is more to the Creator God Elohim than human language can encompass. "In the beginning, God created the heavens and the Earth. The Earth was without form and void, and darkness was over the face of the deep. And the Spirit of God was hovering over the face of the waters" (Genesis 1:1–2).

GRAPPLING WITH THE MYSTERY OF ELOHIM'S NATURE

Unfortunately, as soon as many hear that there is something about Moses' explanation for our origins that is supernatural or beyond the grasp of the human mind, they become disinterested. Secularism automatically rules out the divine, because it doesn't square well with current notions of our purely naturalistic, scientific culture. As soon as the notion of the supernatural is mentioned, many dig in their heels and make an attack on faith as soft, irrational, or illogical. Many secularists act as if faith requires one to reject reason.

But true faith is not blind in the sense that it dismisses reason. Rather, true faith arms reason with a framework—the big picture within which reason operates. An intelligent person of faith examines the evidence to find his or her place within the midst of the all-encompassing story of Elohim's work. Properly understood, faith opens the mind by giving someone the courage to examine things as they are and to consider whether Elohim could have a hand in bringing all things into existence.

Those who dismiss the Genesis narrative before considering the framework it proposes for the origins of the cosmos on its own terms pronounce a guilty verdict before hearing the case. If people lived their lives in contempt of everything they don't already understand, we would live in a world with no cell phones, microwave ovens, or other modern contrivances. If we never ventured to seek new answers to difficult questions, all of science and exploration would quickly die out for fear of the unknown—fear of what's thought to be supernatural.

Human beings have a built-in desire for intellectual growth in understanding the world we live in. Every intellectual pursuit grows from this impulse. One of the most satisfying aspects of life is discovering answers to difficult questions and solving puzzles. Is anyone up for a Sudoku or crossword puzzle?

Admitting God as an option in the quest to understand human origins equips the mind for the pursuit of truth. Those who begin their inquiry into the unknown by dismissing God from the start are intellectually dishonest if they suggest they have considered every possibility. Just as it would be unwise to dismiss technology for lack of understanding, it would be foolish to dismiss God because one can't fully wrap her or his mind around the divine.

Currently, dark energy and dark matter, neither of which has been directly observed, are acceptable explanations for how galaxies hold together. God is no less observable than these mysterious forces. Fear of the inability to intellectually grapple with unknowns doesn't dissuade those who hope to find the truth about their origins. Faith gives courage to look for true answers outside of one's self, test assumed theories, and begin a liberating search for a deeper understanding of reality.

Moses gave the reader just a peek at the creation of all things. His curious introduction to the divine isn't illogical. It's doubly logical. If God is infinite (which implies He is all-powerful, preexisting, and eternal), human language could never hope to encompass the fullness of who He is. Elohim revealed Himself to humanity through Moses' pen so that we may come to a true knowledge of Him, even though we may never fully comprehend Him.

Human language simply isn't equipped with ways to express something that is beyond that which we have already grasped. We can speak poetically, figuratively, and symbolically but never fully express something above and beyond our reason, because we are, by our nature, limited. Elohim, by His nature, is unlimited. Moses (led by the Spirit, who accommodated humanity by moving Moses to record this account in human language) did the best he could to convey the mystery of Elohim in a way that could be communicated, even if it could never be fully comprehended.

KNOW YOUR LIMIT

What would be illogical, when confronted with the divine, would be to try to put Elohim in a box. If He truly is God, then He would be supernatural and thus by His very being above and beyond our reason and senses. We could never realistically hope to fully grasp Him by ascending to heaven via our own intellectual pursuits. Trying to fully unravel and explain the mystery of Elohim would be the same as trying to confine the infinite to something finite. Such is mathematically and logically impossible.

It's time for an illustration. The average brain is somewhat larger than a one-liter bottle (although you may sometimes wonder if this is true with some people). This means that if God is infinite, then comparatively speaking, human beings would have better luck trying to fit all of the water of the Pacific Ocean into a one-liter bottle than being able to fully wrap their brains around Moses' Elohim.

According to the National Oceanic and Atmospheric Administration, the Pacific Ocean, by far the largest ocean on the planet, contains roughly 660 million cubic kilometers of water.[32] This is an unfathomable amount of water. You can say, "660 million." You could sail across this large ocean. You could swim or dive into it. You could take a submarine to its greatest depths. You may even observe most of it in a view from space, but you will never be able to fully comprehend its diversity, depth, or breadth all at once.

Yet as large as the Pacific Ocean is, it comes nowhere close to being infinite. As the earth's largest ocean, it is vitally important to global climate and life on earth, but its mass is insignificant when compared to the mass of the rest of the earth. To further compound matters, the earth is but an insignificant speck in our miniscule solar system, lost in the sea of stars from our own galaxy, which is just one of the billions of galaxies within the known universe. If the Pacific Ocean is only a tiny part of a tiny part of the known universe and we can't wrap our brains around it, how are we supposed to fully grasp Elohim?

It is hard for us to understand the depth of the Pacific Ocean—not to mention the depth of the known universe—yet even these immense spaces are finite. The more we know of the oceans and the further we peer into space, the smaller we feel. Because we are limited, there should be some sense of wonder and mystery when observing that which we can't fully comprehend. Given our limitations in understanding a limited universe, we should be humble when pondering the possibility of an infinite and eternal (and therefore unlimited) Creator.

Moses didn't get lost in the details or try to make the reader understand the entirety of Elohim. He merely introduced Elohim in a way that pointed to His sheer awesomeness and majesty. Had Moses attempted to accurately describe the fullness of Elohim, he would still be writing.[33]

THE MATERIAL REALM IS THE TRULY CREATIVE EXPRESSION OF ELOHIM'S WILL

Without getting bogged down in a detailed explanation of Elohim, Moses began the story of creation and the origins of life by using a Hebrew word for *created* that is only used of Elohim in the entire Hebrew Scriptures. This is important to note, because according to the Scriptures, only Elohim can create from nothing. The Hebrew word for *created* has a twofold meaning. The twin meanings of this word, which has no adequate English equivalent, illustrate well what happened the moment Elohim made everything.

This Hebrew word means "making, molding, or forming something." Think of a potter shaping a vessel from a soft lump of clay or a smith working metal into a tool to get an idea of this sense of the word. When Elohim created, everything was planned and ordered from the start. There would be no unintended mistakes, because it was not possible for Him to make errors. Elohim's creation will accomplish its purpose.

The word for *created* also includes the giving of life. The human body is composed of everything necessary to live, but without the breath of life, it is only a corpse. Elohim gave living things His breath of life, thus animating what He had formed.

Only Moses' Elohim can create by forming that which previously didn't exist and by giving that which He had formed life. Human beings, as creative as they are, don't have the power to bring into existence what did not previously exist. We can rearrange what exists, build with it, or smash it into tiny pieces, but the ability to truly create is reserved for God alone.

It is amazing to see how many ways the human race expresses its creative prowess on the walls of ancient caves, in oil on canvass, and in places of industry, where practical application of invention and innovation are the key components of successful businesses. But the creativity (used loosely here in relation to Elohim's exclusive ability to create) of humans is limited to mastering and reorganizing already existing matter. God, by first creating energy and matter and then combining them in a way that brought life to previously nonexistent clay, is able to do far more than humanity could ever hope or even imagine.

There is a story of a scientist who finally figured out how to create life, so he challenged the necessity of God by saying that the human race no longer needed God. He supposed that because a human could make something alive, God was no longer needed. Much to his surprise, God appeared in his lab one day and asked the scientist to demonstrate how he was able to bring life into being.

The scientist immediately got to work and started by picking up some soil to analyze. He began breaking it down into the components he needed to produce the molecules of the basic self-replicating protein he had managed to synthesize. But as soon as he reached down to pick up the dirt, God stopped the scientist and told him, "Whoa, stop right there! I created that soil; it's mine. You need to make your own dirt!" Such is the difference between humanity's ability to create and Elohim's ability to create.

THE CREATOR DISTINCT FROM HIS CREATION

This brings us to a final consideration of who Elohim is before digging into the creation account itself. According to Moses, Elohim was separate and distinct from His creation. Before Elohim brought light into the abyss, there was nothing except Him. Moses' Elohim is a spiritual being, so He had to create matter and energy in order for His master plan for the universe to unfold.

What human beings are able to perceive through their five senses—the natural realm—is physical and composed solely of matter and energy. Because the Creator is Spirit and His creation is physical, the universe cannot be the Creator. Nor is the Creator the universe.

Moses explained that at the moment of creation, everything came to be where nothing previously was. To the best of our current understanding, that means that the stuff of creation and the natural laws that now govern it all began at the same time—the moment of creation. But before God made His presence known through creation, three words describe what once was where we now are:

- *toe*-who: formlessness, unreality, emptiness.[34] In an empty state, completely devoid of matter.
- va-*bow*-who: and emptiness.[35] Completely void. The absence of anything.

- va-*hoe*-sheck: and darkness, obscurity.[36] Complete darkness, because as yet in the narrative, there is literally nothing and no energy to observe.

With these three words, Moses intentionally distinguished between the Creator and the creation in Genesis. The triple reinforcement of the fact that there was literally nothing of energy or matter—or anything besides Elohim—is unique to Moses' creation story. It offers a clean break from the other ancient accounts popular at his time.

The centrality of God (Elohim) and His exclusive ability to create in Genesis 1 immediately gave way to the act of creation. Why all was created will become clearer as creation is consummated and blessed by Elohim. But before addressing why all was made, it is important to examine how it was formed according to the order of creation as presented by Moses. His account, much like the current secular account, progresses from the cosmic scale to the planetary scale.

What will become clear by the end is that the order of creation proposed by Moses elevates humanity to a place of prominence. Each day of the Genesis account brought the focus of God's work nearer to completion with human beings. According to Moses, life is no cosmic coincidence. By the end of Genesis 1, it will become clear that humanity was the reason why everything was created in the first place.

LET THERE BE LIGHT

There has been much debate about the Genesis creation account, especially whether creation happened in six literal, twenty-four-hour days. When the question of "how long" comes up, it is hard (to say the least) to cram 13.7 billion years into 144 hours. There currently is no compromise position between the literal scriptural interpretation of Genesis 1–2 and the secular explanation of origins, as both make absolute claims based upon facts that appear mutually exclusive of the other.

If the world is indeed billions of years old and the human race is the product of natural selection rather than a special act of creation, then the introductory chapters of the Bible are not true. This would bring into question all of the rest of the Bible. No sensible person would continue to trust another human being whom she or he knew for a fact began a conversation by lying to her or his face and then persisted in those lies. That would be crazy! Why, then, would anyone trust a book—*especially* if it claims to be a holy book—if its introduction is not trustworthy?

Some scientifically-minded Christians, sensitive to the implications of believing in a holy book that is deemed irrelevant by a secular scientific culture, have ventured all sorts of attempts to reconcile the biblical creation account with the theories of secular

science. Thus far, most attempts to find a compromise position
have fallen short. Theistic evolutionists, favoring the secular view
of humanity's origins while trying to retain the moral and spiritual
teachings of the Bible, have dismissed the notion of creation
happening in six literal days.

Some have proposed that the Bible is true in the spiritual and
moral realms but not in its explanation for how things actually
came into being. Their model proposes a Creator who set the ball
rolling eons ago (a notion whose God resembles the God of Deism
more than the Elohim of Moses), who basically stepped back from
His creation until dramatically intervening in human history by
revealing His plan for salvation in the person of His Son, Jesus
Christ. This theology operates under a principle similar to (if not
adopted from) Darwinism, which admits the possible necessity of
a Creator who basically disappears once the laws are in place for
the continuance of existence.

This interpretation poses theological difficulty, especially when
it comes to determining what portions of Scripture are literally
true or not. If the Bible is merely the product of fallible human
authors and can be interpreted metaphorically when no figurative
parable or poetry is introduced as such, the reader gets to determine
what's inspired and what is not. This opens the door to reading
meaning into a text instead of searching for the author's intended
meaning.

If the Genesis—the beginning—didn't happen as described,
how can we be certain that other key portions of Scripture are to
be trusted? Was Jesus a real person or just a mythic figure? Did
He literally, physically rise from the dead? Will there be a bodily
resurrection at the end of time? These are important claims that
the Bible says are true.[37]

But are these claims true in a literal or figurative sense? If
Genesis 1–3 is merely metaphorical, then every claim the Bible
makes could be taken as such and wouldn't really mean anything
in the end. Indeed, all of Christianity could be reduced to pure

mysticism and have nothing to do with the real world we live in if all of Scripture were reduced to spiritual metaphor.

Fundamentalist Christians, holding fast to a literal six-day creation, have struggled to defend the validity of the Genesis in an entirely different way than those who interpret Genesis 1–2 symbolically or metaphorically. Because of their desire to remain true to the traditional Christian view of Scripture, they face a different quandary. They often find themselves entrenched in dogmatic positions that most scientists and many discerning and intelligent Christians openly question.

In the name of orthodoxy, some Christian organizations have tried to defend the biblical model by calling into question much of the science used to support the secular view of human origins. They attack the science supporting the theory of the big bang as the origin of the universe. Some even resort to invoking ancient popular legends and mythology for evidence to defend their beliefs. Finding solace in their beliefs by dismissing science while upholding legends from folklore as possibly true accounts comes off as desperate and silly.

A meaningful and helpful dialogue is only possible with reasonable, rational, and informed people. Those who cling to myth while rejecting science relegate their relevance to an audience that already believes as it does. Grasping at straws, they have pigeonholed themselves by reasoning themselves into a lonely corner.

There is real tension in trying to make sense of what science and the Scriptures propose, because they seem to be completely at odds. This tension has been exacerbated, because both camps, in zeal for their cause, at times appear willing to believe almost anything that contradicts their opponents.

A middle way between the secular camp that views the Scriptures as scientifically irrelevant and a literal interpretation of Genesis 1–2 may be found when one considers who is behind the opening chapters of the Bible. Elohim, as described by Moses in the opening verses, is far above human understanding and not handcuffed by natural laws, as humans are. This means that the laws of physics can't limit Him unless He chooses to be bound by them.

Understanding that what limits humanity is no handicap to Elohim opens the door to the very real possibility that events transpired quickly at the beginning of time when compared to the pace at which natural phenomena currently plod along. Some may, on the basis of principle, deny this suggestion, but they cannot prove it wrong, since no human being was present to observe how all things came to be.

As for those who would dismiss science in favor of a literal rendering of the Genesis account, wouldn't it be better to disagree with the application of scientific data instead of arguing against the science behind the data? True observational science deals only in the realm of observable, reproducible, and therefore verifiable fact, which is hard to argue against. But the interpretation of theories based upon scientific fact is subject to challenge and change.

When taken at face value as a description of the creation of all things, Genesis proposes a model that can't be disproven by secular science or proven true by creationists. No, Genesis does not tell us exactly how everything began in the same way a physics textbook explains the orbits of planets around a star. But it does provide a working pattern for telling how all things have come to be. Despite many arguments to the contrary, the closer secular science comes to a unified explanation of the forces that have formed and sustain the universe, many of the newest theories proposed by leading scientists sound eerily similar to the course of events first proposed by, of all people, Moses.

As we embark on this journey through the creation account, we need to be careful to understand that our discussion will often venture from observable, proven, demonstrated, and tested scientific fact to theoretical science. No one was an eyewitness to what happened when everything came to be, so we are stuck trying to figure out *how it could have happened*. When making illustrations to help the reader better understand his or her origin, the author in no way insists that creation must have been this way or that. Elohim was free to create however He deemed best and inspired Moses to record an accurate description of His creative activity. When reflecting on origins, all are limited to the best current understanding of reality when trying to describe how the universe began.

As is the case with every scientific theory, new information often requires revision of previously accepted scientific fact. We examine Moses' Genesis account in light of what we now know to the best of our ability. Moses' account hasn't changed in 3,500 years. Current theories, apart from Elohim, have evolved through thousands (if not millions) of revisions. In order for a reader who has been brought up on a steady diet of secular scientific theory and vocabulary to have a chance at understanding the Genesis account, we will examine the first chapters of Genesis in light of current scientific thought.

LET THERE BE LIGHT

In the previous chapter, we discussed how intentional Moses was in his insistence that before Elohim spoke, there was literally nothing of the natural realm to be perceived. The triple reinforcement that there was nothing, no space, and complete darkness drove this point home. Even Elohim (a spiritual being) would have been imperceptible to physical creatures until He made Himself known. "In the beginning, God created the heavens and the Earth. The Earth was without form and void, and darkness was over the face of the deep. And the Spirit of God was hovering over the face of the waters. And God said, 'Let there be light,' and there was light" (Genesis 1:1–3).

Moses wrote that at a command, in less than a millisecond, light was created out of nothing. Could this light be a nearly infinite amount of energy released by the Word of God? If so, it could describe a beginning to the universe that closely resembles humanity's best approximation of how everything began with the big bang. Stephen Hawking describes the event that began the universe from a secular perspective: "At the big bang itself the universe is thought to have had zero size, and so to have been infinitely hot. But as the universe expanded, the temperature of the radiation decreased. One second after the big bang, it would have fallen to about ten thousand million degrees."[38] What Hawking proposes is that everything exploded into existence. A release of infinite power would have made the universe experience more change in the first moments and hours after the big bang than it has since.

Many Christians consider it blasphemy to compare the big bang with the moment of creation, but whichever model you follow, both start at the same point. In an instant, everything that would ever be anything came to be in a burst of pure energy. Christians teach that the energy of creation was released at the command of Elohim.

Secularists don't yet have a unanimous explanation why but insist that at the beginning, the universe started with a release of energy within which everything that would become anything was contained. Time itself began in this instant. Space was born. Matter, energy (actually, the energy that would become matter), and the laws of physics came into being. Had any physical being observed this event, it may have appeared from a distance as nothing at first but quickly could have emitted all sorts of energy, heat, and radiation. Another word for photons and radiation is the very word Moses used to describe what was created on the first day—*light*.

Light is a form of energy. It is the form of energy that, in the ancient world, would have best described the moment of creation as currently envisioned by secular science—that is, if (as secular science has now proposed) that at the creation, energy preceded matter. Moses wrote Genesis from the perspective of a distant observer, which may be why he didn't use the word *heat* to describe what happened at the universe's genesis. Light, which is technically photons at wavelengths perceptible to the human eye, best represents *energy*, which is currently thought to have been necessary for the universe to begin.

On this point, Moses' description may very well be compatible with Einstein. In his theory of relativity, Einstein demonstrated mathematically how energy and mass are equivalent. They can be converted one into the other. $E=mc^2$ demonstrates how much energy is contained within mass.

One does well to note that the constant in Einstein's equation is the speed of light, which is time-dependent. (This will become an important consideration later.) Is it a mere coincidence that the speed of light is the constant in this simple equation which is foundational to modern physics? Or did Einstein somehow unintentionally stumble onto an aspect of the fabric of existence that is tied to the creation of light at the very beginning of time?

Even though Moses wrote Genesis more than three thousand years before Einstein was conceived, Moses began his account by describing the release of light. It doesn't seem contrary to reason to assume that this light could be thought of as pure energy. Through the creation of pure energy, Elohim brought light and life—both literally and figuratively—into the darkness.

We will most likely never fully appreciate how much energy was created in the beginning. One does not need to look further than Hiroshima or Nagasaki to see the devastating raw power that is released when mass is converted into energy. At Nagasaki, only about one gram of plutonium was converted back into energy in a fission reaction that leveled the city and killed tens of thousands of people. The opposite of this destructive property of matter (fission) is the creative force that turns energy into mass (fusion). Considering how much energy is released in a nuclear bomb, how much energy was required to create everything that exists? "And God saw that the light was good. And God separated the light from the darkness. God called the light Day, and the darkness he called Night. And there was evening and there was morning, the first day" (Genesis 1:4–5).

HOW DOES LIGHT BECOME MORE THAN LIGHT?

Before you can have a universe, you have to have matter. Before you have matter, you have to have energy that will form the building blocks of matter. The subatomic building blocks of matter include larger hadrons (such as the familiar proton and neutron) and smaller leptons (such as electrons and a whole array of newly discovered and possibly as-yet undiscovered wave-particles). To the best of our current understanding, in a newborn universe, gazillions of super-heated wave-particles would have emitted incredibly high-energy radiation—or *light*.

We can't look any direction in the universe without seeing light. Even the dark places in the night sky are not completely dark; they are merely devoid of visible light. The dark spaces in the night sky that appear empty to the naked eye glow with radiation viewed by telescopes designed to observe longer or shorter wavelengths of radiation than visible light.

We should expect to find light everywhere we look if the universe began as a flash of light. Cosmic background radiation has been admitted as evidence of the big bang. Could it not also be interpreted as the afterglow of an act of creation that began as pure light?

Moses' light may very well be the best possible description of the raw energy that was the universe at the moment of creation. But you can have too much of a good thing. Too much light, or energy, packed into a small space would mean too much heat for life as we know it to develop.

According to current scientific theory, the energy released at the beginning of time was initially condensed in an infinitely small space. We now inhabit a universe that is possibly infinitely large. The physics that help explain how the universe went from infinitesimally small to being potentially infinitely large have been under investigation for some time, and recent observations of the farthest reaches of space have revealed a glimpse at an infantile universe just like what was predicted by big bang theorists.

Universal inflation, which has been observed and is now well-documented, is one more reason some encourage the public to reject creation. But does inflation contradict the pattern of creation described by Moses? Whether creation was planned or not, if the universe was ever to have a chance of giving birth to life, things had to cool down from what is currently believed (by the secular scientific community) to be a nearly infinitely hot beginning. A universe that expanded exponentially would naturally cool everything down.

Does an expanding universe disprove Moses' account? Secular scientists have looked for evidence of an expanding universe to bolster their case against creationists. As they looked outside of our galaxy and mapped its farthest reaches, they discovered that the universe does indeed appear to be expanding, which actually accords quite well with what Moses described happening on the second day of his creation account.

AN EXPANSE IN THE
MIDST OF THE WATERS

It is quite likely that people have always pondered life and existence when looking to the heavens. Even though humanity has often wondered about the realm above, we have only managed to touch the surface of the expanse above us. Even with telescopes powerful enough to peer billions of miles into space, we have only just begun to know what lies out there.

The twentieth century saw a revolution in the study of the heavens. In one generation, humanity became aware of galaxies outside of our own for the first time, learned of the expansion of the universe, landed a manned mission on the moon, and developed technologies that allowed us to see deeper into space and in colors never seen before. This technological revolution fueled an explosion in knowledge that completely rewrote our understanding of the opening chapter of the book of life.

HUMANITY'S UNDERSTANDING OF THE
HEAVENS EXPANDED EXPONENTIALLY

Edwin Hubble was the first person to observe galaxies outside of our own. When he did, he noticed that galaxies weren't fixed in particular places. They appeared to move away from earth. This observation was not what many of his contemporaries expected, because to the unaided eye, stars (many of which are actually galaxies outside our own) appear to remain stationary in the night sky.

Back in the 1920s, Hubble measured the speed at which he observed galaxies moving away from earth. Logic dictates that if galaxies move away from Earth at a set speed, by mathematically reversing the motion, astronomers should be able to determine how long ago everything was all in one place. Hubble's observations of the known universe at his time seemed to indicate that the universe was about 1.5 billion years old.[39]

That's far too old, according to young earth creationists, and far too young, according to secular astronomers today, but that estimation was the best Hubble could make with the data and technology of the time. Most importantly, it provided evidence for an expanding universe. The application of inflation theory and a much improved picture of space have since had profound effects on our current view of the birth of the universe.

INFLATION LEADS TO A CALMER, KINDER UNIVERSE

Current theory regarding the origin of the universe is built upon the concept of universal inflation. The basic premise is that if all of the energy and matter of the entire universe were contained within an infinitely small space at the beginning, then immediately following the birth of the universe, the repulsive forces of matter would force everything out and away from the center. All of the tightly packed energy formed in the moment of creation (that has now become everything we observe in the universe), condensed into an infinitely small space, would have glowed "white hot." [40] As such, everything would have been unstable until it expanded and cooled.

To test the theory of inflation and measure the accuracy of the current inflationary model of the universe, NASA launched the Wilkinson Microwave Anisotropy Probe (WMAP) in 2001 on a nearly decade-long mission to map the furthest reaches of space.

Every two years, the probe mapped the universe in every direction. The hope was to take a detailed "baby picture of the universe" that would reveal what conditions were like when the universe was an estimated 375,000 years old.[41]

There is much excitement about the findings of the WMAP mission, because the image of the universe as it was at an estimated age of 375,000 years is as far back into the history of the universe people may ever be able to see. To put into perspective how young a universe this picture represents, we can compare it to a baby picture of an elderly adult. A hundred-year-old person has lived about 36,524 days. Dividing 13.77 billion years by 36,524 equals 377,012 years. In other words, if 13.77 billion years were reduced to a mere hundred years, 375,000 years would equate to about one day of life. Figuratively speaking, the WMAP mission has provided a snapshot into the first "day" in the life of the universe.

A number of important assumptions that form the basis of current secular theory about the nature of the early universe were verified by data collected in the WMAP mission. Among the most important concepts confirmed is the idea that "the universe underwent a dramatic early period of expansion, growing by more than a trillion trillion-fold in less than a trillionth of a trillionth of a second."[42] As hard as it is to imagine, both the scriptural and secular stories of the universe's origin agree that everything that would ever be anything was formed the moment space was born.

With everything literally squeezed into an infinitely small space at the beginning, the repulsive forces between subatomic particles drove the universe to expand. They appear to have done so in a way that made the birth of galaxies possible, because "tiny fluctuations were generated during this expansion that eventually grew to form galaxies."[43] This observation of an expanding and varied infantile universe was hailed as good news for those who believe the big bang theory and can also be taken as good news for those who believe in a divine act of creation.

Had the infant cosmos been perfectly uniform and all of the forces perfectly balanced each other, it would have been much more unlikely for any significant structure, like galaxies, to form. In a perfectly uniform universe, all of the forces of physics may very well have balanced and therefore cancelled each other out. Was variation in the fabric of the newborn universe a fortunate coincidence? Or could Elohim have designed His creation this way to allow for stability in cosmic neighborhoods that would become hospitable for the development of life?

Ripples, or wrinkles, in the young universe help to explain why the current universe has regions filled with observable matter and other places where there appears to be an absence of matter. If life was to develop, there couldn't have been too much energy or matter crammed into such a small space forever. But at the same time, there had to be enough material somewhere in order for something to come into existence if life was to be a possibility.

Varying densities of matter throughout space show one aspect of the physical realm that makes it much more likely that life would emerge somewhere in the cosmos. But at the same time, this reality also cancels out any chance for life in about 99.9999999999 percent of the universe. It appears that we have beaten the odds.

From Inflation to the Elements

If inflation generated the space for the current universe, it also made the matter that comprises the known universe possible. Had the energy of creation remained in an infinitely small space, everything could have collapsed upon itself, or an entirely different reality than the physical one we inhabit could have developed. Humanity is handicapped in speculation about other possible directions the universe could have taken, because our understanding is limited to what can be physically observed.

When we forget what could have been and focus on what we can observe, it seems apparent (in light of the WMAP observations) that in about 1/36,720th of the time creation has existed, atoms could have begun to form. Current models show how the raw energy of the big bang may have been settled down during inflation as the nearly infinite amount of energy released in an infinitely small space immediately spread out. According to this model, it would have taken a relatively short amount of time for sub-subatomic particles to cool to the point that they bound together to form the building blocks of atoms. As temperatures continued to fall to what we currently observe in stars, atoms would have begun forming, and fusion of atoms into heavier elements would have begun.

Under normal circumstances observed in stars, the simplest elements—hydrogen, helium, and lithium—are the first to form. Most stars, for most of their lives, burn hydrogen by fusing it into helium. Helium can then fuse with another hydrogen atom to form lithium, or it can fuse with other helium atoms to form carbon. Carbon fuses into oxygen, and up the periodic table until iron and the heaviest elements are formed.

By the time iron and the heaviest elements are formed in a star, it is doomed to die. Stars die when their gravity overpowers fusion; the star collapses upon itself and explodes in a supernova. It is the most violent—and possibly most beautiful—natural phenomena astronomers can observe today. Supernovae's leftovers (nebulae) seed the universe with the raw material for new stars and solar systems to form, complete with a variety of elements necessary to produce life.

Current secular theory suggests that only hydrogen, helium, and trace amounts of lithium were formed at the birth of the universe, because the universe expanded so fast that fusion was halted until stars were born. Depending on how hot it was and how long it took the energy and matter of the universe to separate, it is not inconceivable that in the very beginning, atoms were fused into heavier elements. Although heavier elements account for only a minute amount of the total matter in the known universe, they are absolutely essential to the development of life, because organic beings (such as humans) are made up of carbon and are dependent upon oxygen and a host of other elements.

Right now, we observe an abundance of light elements and only miniscule amounts of the heavier elements that are necessary for life. Considering the insanely high pressure, temperature, and energy of a young universe, if the inconceivably immense forces at work in creation created pockets of greater pressure or heat, heavier elements could have been created in a similar fashion to how they are formed today in dying stars. For life to emerge on Earth before 10 billion years or so passed in the universe, only a relatively tiny amount of organic and heavier elements (enough to allow life to sprout in only one place in the universe) needed to be formed in the beginning.

Could the wrinkles of WMAP's baby picture of the universe suggest this is possible? All it would have taken for heavier elements to form would be regions in the infant universe to remain dense enough (and therefore hot enough) for fusion to take place before stars were born. Considering that according to current theory, everything that exists was contained in a nearly infinitely small point, this wouldn't be impossible. Fusion taking place before the birth of stars could easily explain why a young universe that only has sparse amounts of heavier elements could birth a relatively young earth that is so organic and rich with heavier elements.

Why would it be irrational to propose that fusion may have happened at the very beginning of time in an environment that was as close as scientists can conceive to what is now observed in the interior of a star? Current theory insists that the infantile universe wasn't uniform. Could the energetic matter of creation have been rippled by intense forces that travelled through space like a rock hitting a pond or a fish swimming in water? If ripples in the fabric of space created fluctuating densities and temperature, then pockets of space that had once cooled enough for atoms to stabilize may very well have been heated up to the point of fusion and then cooled again.

There is no telling how many times and in how many places this rippling of space may have happened allowing organic and heavier elements to be created at the beginning of time. Such a theory, as difficult as it would be to prove, does provide a mechanism for the raw ingredients of life to be created at the beginning of the universe. In an infinite universe, even if the window of opportunity was brief, such rippling events could have taken place an infinite number of times. This being the case, one could theorize that it wouldn't have taken long at all, from a cosmic perspective, for conditions to become suitable for the development of stars, planets, and in at least one place, life—complete with elements necessary for life, including carbon, oxygen, iron, and all the rest.

THE EXPANSE ABOVE THE EARTH

Very early in Moses' description of creation, a particular part of the cosmos received special attention from Elohim. According to Moses, on the second day, Elohim set some of what He had created apart: "And God said, 'Let there be an expanse in the midst of the waters, and let it separate the waters from the waters. And God made the expanse and separated the waters that were under the expanse from the waters that were above the expanse. And it was so. And God called the expanse Heaven. And there was evening and there was morning, the second day" (Genesis 1:6–8).

What was set apart, according to Moses, was the part of the cosmos we call home—the earth. The matter that would become humanity was hitherto indistinguishable from the rest of what Elohim had created on the first day. Now it was separated and shielded, because out of all the matter of the universe, this would be the particular place, and this would be the specific stuff, from which humanity would be formed.

The primordial earth, as described by Moses, appears to have been a very fluid place. In order for life to arrive sooner than later, the raw materials for life were ordered and arranged for creatures to be formed and thrive. If the early solar system was anything like it is pictured by astronomers, the young planet would also need to be shielded from the cosmic bombardment of radiation and space debris before life could emerge. An expanse separating earth from space provided both of these necessities.

The Hebrew word translated as "expanse" could include everything of the heavens we now divide into the lower and upper atmosphere, but it ends where space begins.[44] This expanse, atmosphere, or heaven was set into place before life emerged to accomplish the important task of shielding life. One of the features of earth that sets it apart from the other planets as a place particularly well-suited for life is her atmosphere. One needs look no further than the two nearest neighbors in our solar system to see how important it is to have just the right atmosphere.

Venus has too much surface pressure and an atmosphere that's composed of the wrong stuff for oxygen-breathing, water-filled life forms to live. Her primarily carbon dioxide atmosphere is very acidic and creates unbearable surface temperatures. Venus's surface is so hot that the few space probes that have descended through her acidic atmosphere were most likely cooked and melted shortly after descent.

The atmospheric pressure on Venus is also ninety times what is experienced here on earth.[45] Although life may someday be discovered there, it is quite unlikely that anything living there is dependent upon liquid water and oxygen. Liquid water would immediately evaporate in such a place. The combination of unbearable pressure, temperature, and acidity is a Venusian recipe for death, not life.

Mars, on the other hand, has an atmosphere without enough breathable oxygen or surface pressure to be conducive to human life. Although it is theoretically possible that at some point in the future, liquid water could be found on the surface of Mars (depending on how industrious and ingenious our children and grandchildren prove to be), so far, none has been found. Combine the lack of an appreciable amount of water and oxygen with the danger posed by asteroids that often fall to the planet's surface, and you have another environment currently inhospitable to life.

These two examples show that atmosphere is absolutely essential for life to develop. This is possibly why the expanse is the first feature of the newborn earth described in the Genesis account. Space (meaning the distance between earth and her cosmic neighbors) is also very important.

SPACE = SAFE!

From a cosmological perspective, there are many benefits of being separated by great distances from others. If we begin a reflection on our place in space by looking to the other planets of our own solar system, we see that all of our planetary neighbors are at very safe distances from us. The smaller inner planets are tens of millions of miles away. The larger outer planets are hundreds of millions of miles away. These are kept safely away from the earth by the sun, which holds the planets in very stable (even if somewhat elliptical) orbits on roughly the same plane as the earth's orbit.

The greatest danger from within our own solar system is from asteroids, most of which are far too small to survive a cascade through the earth's atmosphere. Of those that are big enough to cause global harm, including those that get close enough for us to observe, the vast majority never cross our path. Halley's Comet, at its closest approach to earth in AD 837, was over 3 million miles away.[46] Back in 1997, the world witnessed the Hale-Bopp Comet, which was one of the brightest objects ever observed in the night sky. Impressive as it was, it never got as close to the earth as the sun.[47]

Earth colliding with another planet or large asteroids would be bad for life on its surface. A collision with a star, on the other hand, could wipe out the earth, the sun, and the entire solar system. To see how likely this could be in the immediate future, we can measure the distance to local stars and see how safe we are. When we measure the safety of our solar system in distance from other stars, we discover that we are in a very safe place once again. Our sun doesn't have many nearby galactic neighbors. As a matter of fact, one would have to travel some 26 trillion miles to even reach our sun's nearest stellar neighbor, Alpha Centauri.[48]

That distance is a hurdle for those who may wish to try interstellar travel. But this is quite a good thing for humans and all of the other earthbound life forms with which we share our planet. Space between cosmic neighbors protects us from potentially harmful effects of things like being ripped away from our sun by the gravitational force of a large neighbor; collision with another celestial body that would undoubtedly destroy our fragile planet; or insanely intense radiation and heat that would make it impossible for anything like us fleshy, fluid-filled creatures to keep from being boiled alive. None of these scenarios would be fun or beneficial to any life form, let alone conducive to the survival of advanced life forms.

To further isolate the earth from danger, she is kept at a very safe distance from other celestial bodies, because our solar system inhabits a remote place even within our own galaxy. Our galaxy, the Milky Way, is a spiral galaxy that is believed to be home to hundreds of billions of stars. Most of these stars are densely crowded in the middle bulge of the galaxy.

The further one travels from the center bulge, the greater the separation between the stars. As one travels from the center of the galaxy and down the arms that extend out and around our galaxy's core, space gets less crowded. Our solar system is located about two-thirds to three-fourths of the way from the galaxy's center on one of these arms. This means that we are in a fairly remote corner of the universe—nowhere near the center of even our own galaxy. The distance from the center of the galaxy is one more reason that earth's place in space is a safe place.

By the end of the second day in Moses' story, the matter that would become the sun and the earth was as yet unformed, but it was beginning to take shape in a safe place. Moses ended the second day with the solar system and earth in an infant state of development, looking an awful lot like what secular science currently proposes a young cosmos and young planet earth looked like. But, there's still the sticky issue of time, especially the length of time necessary for these events to take place.

If every Genesis day were a billion years, that would still be far too short a time, according to current cosmological estimates, for all of these things to take place. This begs the question: could one find the opposing timeframes of the secular and scriptural accounts to somehow be compatible without denying demonstrable scientific fact or the Scriptures?

Only a Matter of Time?

So far, the events described on the first and second day in Genesis generally follow patterns suggested by current cosmologists in their attempts to explain the origin of the universe apart from Elohim. Or, one could say that the pattern suggested by current cosmologists seems to agree, at least in principle, with the order suggested by Moses. He did, after all, publish his account 3,500 years before they invented their model. If this is the case, the biggest difference between these two competing ideologies seems not to be the order in which things happened but how long it took for the universe to take its current shape. Moses claimed that all energy and matter, under divine guidance, came to existence in two days.

Theoretical cosmologists estimate that the big bang happened about 13.77 billion years ago and suggest that since then, the laws of physics have shaped the universe of today.[49] Supporting secular assertions is the current composition of elements in the observed universe.[50] Telescopes and other instruments that can now observe and measure objects billions of light years away from earth pile up data that ever more refines and perfects current models of the universe. This bolsters the secular assertion that the universe appears to be 13.77 billion years old.

Could the difficulty of reconciling Genesis with what is currently observed in the universe be caused by our perspective of time being skewed somehow? We know how fast the clock ticks now at our particular place in time. But if relativity has proven that time is slowed down the closer you get to the speed of light, is it wise to assume that everything everywhere for all of natural history has plodded along at our pace?

If you look up the definition of time in the dictionary, you will find that time isn't a force and doesn't have any power at all. According to *Merriam-Webster,* time is "A nonspatial continuum in which events occur in apparently irreversible succession from the past through the present to the future. b. An interval separating two points on this continuum, measured by selecting a regularly recurring event, as the sunrise, and counting the number of its occurrences during the interval: DURATION. c. A number, as of years, days or minutes, representing such an interval."[51] Simply put, time is a measurement—nothing more. It is the counting of a repeating pattern of natural events that is useful for plotting, planning, and studying things that happen.

Experience proves that it is unwise to assume that time is constant. If time is not some inviolable force but may be bent (or is not as constant, as we once thought), it is important for us to keep these facts in mind when looking at the first six days of creation. Even though we intellectually know better, humanity has a tendency to view time as an inviolable force. We view it as a constant.

From the current human perspective, it seems that time keeps rolling along at a steady speed. Our lives are framed by time. Time helps us organize and order our affairs. We are born on a particular date at a certain point in time, live for a period of time, and die on our last days. But relativity, the theory upon which most of our current understanding is built, has demonstrated that time is not the constant force that humans have long thought it is.

You may not believe that time is flexible. Consider just one of the ways humanity is forced to deal with the very real effects of time dilation anticipated by Einstein's relativity. Global Positioning System (GPS) satellites are programmed to account for the difference in the passage of time between your GPS unit on the ground and GPS satellites in orbit. GPS systems need to be recalibrated constantly, because time itself has actually slowed down for satellites due to the speed of their fall in orbit. Time dilation is scientifically proven to be true. If the cesium clock in a GPS satellite isn't recalibrated based upon its speed and altitude, it is impossible for your GPS device to pinpoint your exact location.

The difference in the passage of time between the surface of the earth and an orbiting satellite is far too small to be perceptible to an observer who watched an earthbound clock and the display of a GPS satellite's clock side-by-side. But if neither clock was recalibrated, after a few years, you would begin to see the difference in time. After about seventy years without adjustment, the two clocks would be a whole second different. The real-life application of this concept is that if the clocks on GPS satellites weren't recalibrated constantly, the real difference in time between satellites and ground-based devices would quickly accumulate to the point that your receiver would no longer be able to triangulate your position, and you would be lost!

Science has predicted and calculated the flexibility of time in light of relativity. The Scriptures also testify to the flexible nature of time. The psalmist described the relativity of time from God's perspective: "For a thousand years in your sight are but as yesterday when it is past, or as a watch in the night" (Psalm 90:4). The apostle Peter reiterated this sentiment in his second epistle: "But do not overlook this one fact, beloved, that with the Lord one day is as a thousand years, and a thousand years as one day" (2 Peter 3:8). Recognizing that the Scriptures testify that time isn't constant and science has demonstrated the same, Christians should be better equipped to deal with some of the apparent contradictions between Scripture's timeframe of creation and science's current best estimates.

That being said, there are two wrong ways to attempt to reconcile the time differences between secular and scriptural explanations of our origins. One mistake is to throw away what the Scriptures describe without trying to understand it within its context or frame of reference. The opposite mistake is to dismiss, purely on the basis of religious grounds, any attempt to grow in an understanding of how things could have taken their current shape based upon our best scientific understanding of how the universe operates now.

There are many ways to apply scientific advancement for the betterment of life without denying Elohim or the Scriptures. Although it is difficult to balance the different perspectives of time according to science and the Scriptures, it is essential if a reasonable person of faith hopes to come to the best possible understanding of reality. A good dose of humility will go a long way toward achieving this goal.

Martin Luther, in his Genesis commentary, wrote:

> What will you assume to have been outside time or before time? Or what will you imagine that God was doing before there was any time? Let us, therefore, rid ourselves of such ideas and realize that God was incomprehensible in His rest before the creation of the world, but that now, after the creation, He is within, without, and above all creatures; that is, He is still incomprehensible. Nothing else can be said, *because our mind cannot grasp what lies outside time* (emphasis added).[52]

As helpful as time is for understanding the workings of the natural realm, it can interfere with our attempts to understand an incomprehensible God.

THE GOLDFISH DILEMMA

One illustration that helps us see our limitation of coming to a complete understanding of the universe due to our misconceptions of time is that of a goldfish in a bowl. The illustration works best if we envision a bowl with two rounded sides and two flat sides. The goldfish in such a bowl may see the other creatures of his home through the clear glass of the bowl, but his perception will never be perfectly clear or accurate.

If a human stands opposite the glass on a rounded side of the bowl, she could look incredibly tall and skinny in comparison to her actual height/width proportions. (Some would certainly appreciate a taller, leaner appearance!) The goldfish would clearly see things like color (inasmuch as a goldfish can see color) and vaguely recognize different parts of the person, but proportions would certainly be stretched, to say the least. The goldfish may come to recognize the person and would most likely eventually learn through behavioral modification that people equal food. However, shapes and relative sizes would be completely distorted by the rounded shape of the glass.

If a cat sits on the shelf next to the goldfish bowl opposite a flat side of the fishbowl, the cat would also be perceived, but much more accurately. Proportions would be much more true to life. Were the goldfish to try to draw comparisons between the human and cat based upon his perceptions from within the bowl, he would make a host of incorrect suppositions because his perception of reality outside the bowl would be warped by the glass he peered through.

Time has a similar effect upon even our best attempts to determine the true nature of existence outside of our place in it. We can make observations and deduce how things may have taken their current shape based upon reality as we now perceive it. The accuracy of such hypotheses will always be limited by our technology, our intellect, and the state of the universe at our point in time. To compound our dilemma, we have no way to know if, when we attempt to look back in time through our theories and telescopes, we are looking through the flat side of our fish bowl or the rounded side.

To make matters even more frustrating, we are trapped within time! A goldfish isn't as trapped within his environment as we are currently trapped within time. The fish could try to jump out of his bowl to get a better look at the world. But if he is unlucky, he would either suffocate or find out what the true hopes of his fuzzy feline neighbor always were, gulp!

We don't have the luxury of escaping the confines of time in this life. We are stuck in the eternal present. No human being has ever lived in the past, and no human being will ever live in the future. All we have or ever will know is now. We are, in a sense, prisoners of time. Our best current understanding of the nature of existence is also framed within current natural notions of time.

We can't help this or change it. So when trying to answer questions about our origins, we must recognize the limitation time lays on even our best explanations of our origins. Maybe someday, this will no longer be true of our species, but as of right now, this is one handicap we cannot conquer.

CURRENT SECULAR MODELS OF THE UNIVERSE ARE TIME-DEPENDENT

It is important to recall that the one constant in Einstein's equation summarizing the theory of relativity is the speed of light. Speed is a function of distance traveled over time. This means that the foundational theory to our understanding of the workings of the universe is time-dependent. Time has been woven into the fabric of every current explanation of the physical realm and all current secular theories about origins.

The age and size of the universe is determined by observations of space; currently, the estimation of the universe's age and size is based on the assumption that light travels, suspended in time, at a standard speed. If it is discovered that light or particles are somehow able to travel faster than the speed of light, then that would mean photons or particles could actually travel backward in time! Humanity would then have to rethink all current theories about how long it has taken for us to arrive on the cosmic scene.

Scientists are currently studying the particles and energy released when atoms are broken down (using modern particle accelerators and supercolliders), hoping to grasp a fuller understanding of how the universe holds together. This exploration in quantum mechanics has opened windows into how the forces we observe in the universe operate, including time. As theorists delve deeper and deeper into the forces that hold all things together, strange realities such as antimatter, the wave-particle duality of subatomic particles, and other concepts that couldn't have even been conceived before Einstein become foundational to current explanations of how the universe began.

To the best of our current understanding, light is suspended in time, but at least one experiment at CERN (the largest particle accelerator in the world) has indicated that there may be particles that travel faster than the speed of light.[53] If this proves true, that means that previously unknown phenomena could completely rewrite our science textbooks, just as relativity did in the twentieth century. Possible ways that the discovery of particles traveling faster than the speed of light could affect our view of the world include, but are not limited to, the following:

- If photons are found to travel faster than the speed of light, then we will not see the universe as it once was billions of years ago. Instead, we could be seeing the universe as it exists now or possibly as it will exist in the future.
- A foundation for a new understanding of the relationship between space and time, where time is no longer considered the fourth dimension of the known universe, could emerge.
- Relativity (or the lack thereof) could render time irrelevant and possibly even prove that our conceptualization of time is a hurdle in our quest for understanding the true nature of existence.

Try as hard as we might, since we don't even know what the future of our understanding of time is, we can't anticipate the effects of timeless models of the universe. For now, we will continue our journey through the days of creation irrespective of time to see if what Moses proposed way back when could still provide a reasonable basis for understanding how life and humanity came to be.

LET THE EARTH
BRING FORTH

If time is relative and therefore flexible (and possibly even a handicap in our best attempts to make sense of our origins apart from Elohim), then before rejecting the Genesis account, it makes sense to examine Moses' creation story in its entirety. Twentieth-century advancements in the sciences, especially Einstein's theory of relativity, and our deeper awareness of the universe have led secular science down one main line of thought regarding the beginning of the universe—the big bang model. This model has been placed in opposition to the creation account of Genesis.

When one puts the bickering between secular and creationist scientists aside, many similarities in the two creation accounts become apparent. According to secular science, the universe leapt into existence in the release of an infinite amount of energy (light). Moses proposed that, in the beginning, light was created by the power of Elohim's Word.

Secularists propose that inflation caused the energy of creation to quickly cool as it spread out into the matter of the universe. Moses wrote that Elohim formed an expanse in the midst of His creation by separating some of the substance of the universe on the second day to form the earth. Thinking along these lines, it is conceivable that a young universe could hold the possibility for life sooner than later. Such a possibility becomes more of a probability when one considers that the limitations time puts on human theories don't apply to Elohim.

But thus far, only the first two days of creation have been covered. For most scientifically-minded people out there, the question "How long?" is just as important as "How?" It seems that it is easier for many to concede that time may have moved slower (relatively speaking, from our viewpoint) when all of the energy and stuff of creation was spreading out at close to the speed of light. Once there was an earth, time becomes an even more divisive part of the equation, because when examining the geological record, it appears to most that proof of the passage of millions and billions of years has been preserved in the rocks.

The previous chapter began a look at the limitations time puts on the best attempts to discover human origins. Recognizing the limitations of being trapped in the eternal present provides one reason to at least consider Moses' account. If Genesis is to have even a chance of acceptance, it must be noted that evidence from the past can only be examined as it now is, never as it once was. This can be frustrating, because it puts limitations on even the best attempts to understand human beginnings. In the spirit of discovery, it is essential for preconceived notions to take a back seat, or else those who hope to find the truth could inadvertently blind themselves to the truth.

That being said, it would be unfortunate to use the limitation of being trapped in the eternal present as reason to discourage scientists from trying to discover how all things may have come to be. Some Christians have rejected scientific inquiry into such matters in an attempt to defend God from His critics. Such an attitude denies reason, intelligence, and curiosity.

If Christians can apply science and learning to come to a better understanding of human origins and humanity's place in creation, they will have a great advantage when trying to answer the most important questions about existence. Recognizing that a healthy awareness of self comes from a holistic understanding of the world within which one lives, it is important for all to consider the implications of differing worldviews. To help us gain a deeper understanding of the Christ-centered, scriptural worldview, this chapter recounts Moses' record as a literal account of God's deliberately planned creative work. Considering it within its own context while pondering how it relates to what is known about the world brings readers one step closer to discovering what Moses thought of human origins, who people are, and what their place is in creation.

ONE STEP BACK, TWO STEPS FORWARD

Secular models need millions and billions of years to work, because they lack the attention of a powerfully involved creator. According to Moses' description, Elohim planned creation and was active in bringing it to a finished state now, not later. As Darwin himself noted, it would take thousands or even tens of thousands of generations for a species to evolve into another wholly distinct and separate species.[54] If one or two steps in the evolutionary process take thousands of generations, then it would have taken thousands upon thousands (if not millions upon millions or even billions upon billions) of generations before modern humans could arrive on the global scene.

The work of creation, according to Moses, happened in six days. One could say this is because Moses knew nothing of natural selection or how the heavier elements necessary for life are naturally formed in supernovae. These are not the reasons why his account takes so little time. His version of the creation story is quick and to the point for a variety of reasons that are not limited to those listed below:

- Elohim is omnipotent, or all-powerful, which means He created in His own timeframe, however He chose.

- Elohim didn't need to wait for the raw material for His creation to be produced by natural processes, because He could have created the material and the natural processes together in dramatic fashion at the beginning.
- Elohim is omniscient, or all-knowing. This means that everything done in regard to His creation was carefully planned and done right the first time. No thousands of attempts were necessary to get everything just right. Thousands of successive generations were not needed to evolve and tweak organisms in order for them to work in perfect harmony within their ecosystems.
- Elohim created a planet and universe that was ready for life.
- Elohim gave everything a rest when He was done creating. As soon as His initial creative work was complete, it may appear that geological processes were slowed down. Giving the earth a rest could explain how processes that, at today's rate of change, would take thousands or millions of years to happen could have occurred much quicker in the beginning.
- Each step, or day, in creation is complete and contains within itself all that is necessary for the next day. This means that each one of Moses' days contains what current cosmological and evolutionary models propose would have taken millions or billions of years, as the following diagram illustrates.

Seven days of creation in a nutshell

God creates...		God fills what was created with life:	
Day One	Light and dark, called "day" and "night"	Heavenly bodies—sun, moon and stars	Day Four
Day Two	The waters above, "heavens" and waters below, material of earth	All creatures which live in the waters above or below —everything with fins or wings	Day Five
Day Three	Dry land, the seas and all plant life	Land animals, consummated with creation of mankind	Day Six

Day Seven—God gives everything a "rest,"
the first holy-day or "holiday"

There is a carefully-planned progression evident in the seven days of creation. Every day following the first brought what was created on previous day(s) to a further state of development. Symbolically, this is heard in the repetitive, "And there was evening and there was morning..."

THE CONTINENTS EMERGE

Secular theories presuppose that blind forces brought everything to its current state through constant natural processes. Moses described an infinite Elohim bringing everything to its current state very quickly. It isn't hard to imagine (with Elohim involved) that as soon as the creative work of the first day was finished, all of the matter of the universe could have been collected and settled into galactic neighborhoods. This very well may have been when the earth was placed in a nice little cul-de-sac all her own, our solar system. With the stuff of earth congealed and beginning to take shape on the second day, on the third day, the surface of earth became rigid and ready to support life.

The earth had steadily progressed from an indistinguishable place in the midst of a shapeless everything to a very fluid and changing place. The expanse of the heavens protected her from dangerous radiation and outside interference by space. It was time for her to solidify and become rigidly stable so that she could support life.

Continents emerged on the third day. Whether they formed a great supercontinent Pangaea that was later split by the movement of tectonic plates or the continents assumed roughly their current shape and location in the beginning isn't addressed by Moses. What mattered most in his account was that the once fluid place of infantile earth became solid enough to give life a place to be planted.

It is hard for many to believe that a freshly formed planet could cool so that it would be hospitable to life in such a short matter of time. This may be because the earth seems huge, mountains seem immovable, and the seas are too great for human beings to fathom. Humanity can't help but consider these things constant (much like time) and naturally imagine that continents can only change at the slow rates currently observed today.

Although experience teaches that history is punctuated by sudden and drastic changes, humanity seems to find some comfort in imagining that everything has only ever slid along at current rates of change. Many people are uncomfortable with sudden and drastic changes, because they can be threatening. Thinking about disastrous volcanoes such as Krakatoa, Vesuvius, and Mount St. Helens is unsettling. These disasters are insignificant compared with the forces at work to make the earth habitable for humanity. The Indian Ocean tsunami of 2004 and tsunami that hit Japan in 2011 were terrible human tragedies, but the forces that caused them wouldn't have been noticed at an early point in the earth's history.

Holding to notions of a static rate of change may offer some a false sense of security but hinder a deeper understanding of Moses' Elohim and how He could do so much in so little time. In order to cognitively jump over the hurdle of picturing the earth as a mostly static place ruled by slow geologic change, it is very helpful to compare the earth to more familiar things that are easier to comprehend.

OUR INCREDIBLY THIN-SKINNED PLANET

You've heard the dangers of walking on thin ice. You may have had the uncomfortable experience of walking on eggshells. Well, if you were able to slice open the earth and examine it to the core, you would find out that the ground you walk on is, comparatively speaking, much thinner than ice. Compare the earth's crust to eggshells, and you will find that even eggshells are proportionally many times thicker than most of the earth's crust.

When you compare the thickness of the crust to the earth's diameter, you discover a startling reality about the precariousness of life on the surface. According to the United States Geological Survey (USGS), the average thickness of the earth's crust under the United States territories varies between five and six kilometers (below most of the ocean floor) and is as much as sixty kilometers thick under the Sierra Nevadas.[55] Globally, only at the crust's thickest point, under the Himalayas, is the earth's crust more than seventy kilometers thick.[56]

That sounds like lots of crust until comparing these thicknesses to the diameter of the earth, which is about 12,700 kilometers.[57] Divide the thickness of the crust by the diameter of the earth, and one discovers that the crust under the oceans is only about 0.04 percent of the diameter of the earth. Even where the crust is believed to be the thickest, it is less than about 0.6 percent of the total diameter of the earth.

Since those numbers are so small, they are hard to imagine. These percentages can be put into perspective by comparing them to the thickness of an eggshell. Turkish researchers measured all different sizes of eggs and came up with an average shell thickness of about 0.8 percent of an egg's diameter.[58] As a percentage of average diameter, that's twenty times as thick as the vast majority of the earth's crust! Even at its very thickest point under the Himalayas, the earth's crust (as a percentage of the earth's diameter) isn't as thick as an eggshell.

Another way to wrap the mind around the fragility of the earth's crust is to compare its thickness to a ream of paper. In a standard ream of paper, there are five hundred sheets. One sheet of paper is 1/500th of the ream, or 0.2 percent of the thickness of the ream.

In order to demonstrate how thin the earth's crust is under the oceans with one sheet of paper (which is about two-thirds to three-fourths of the earth's crust), five reams of paper are needed. Stack the five reams on top of each other. The top single sheet of paper from that five-ream pile is roughly equivalent to the thickness of the crust under the oceans. That's only one sheet of paper from a stack that is about ten inches tall!

So what's the big deal? The big deal is that seismology and other geosciences have shown that the earth is *not* the big, solid ball of rock and metal, floating around in space, that many imagine it to be. It may appear to be solid from our limited perspective, because the ground is hard, and mountains seem immovable. It would be much more accurate to describe the earth as a dynamic, fluid-filled ball that is covered by a relatively thin layer of solidified rock than to imagine it is a hard ball of rock and metal.

Because the earth's crust is so thin, the rock on the earth's surface didn't need to harden and be shaped over billions of years, as currently suggested. Rather, it could have been formed and cooled quickly. This is made even more likely if water (which has an incredible propensity to cool hot things quickly) found itself on the surface shortly after creation.

Elohim could have quickly extinguished the surface of a fireball of a young earth with the addition of water if He so chose. That opens the possibility that the very same day continents emerged, they were ready for plant life. One might give Moses' Genesis account a double bonus when considering that if Elohim decided to mold the earth in this way, the evaporating water could have turned an inhospitable atmosphere creature-friendly in a hurry! The atmosphere could have been further enhanced for life by gasses released when the rocky surface hardened. This could give a window into a possible interpretation of Genesis 2:6: "and a mist was going up from the land and was watering the whole face of the ground."

The "intellectually" lazy way to describe how this is possible may be to say, "God just made everything the way that it is." ("Intellectually lazy" is what some secularists propose any notion of creationist thought to be.)[59] Moses described Elohim as being more powerful than we could ever hope to understand. If this is true, He could lift the continents and settle the oceans into place with no more difficulty than a small child would have shaping a lump of modeling clay into a ball. Elohim could also contour the earth just as easily as a ten-year-old could press her thumb into a lump of clay.

These illustrations offer a much more accurate depiction of the earth than most current models. They demonstrate how, with just a little imagination and a better understanding of the world we live on (thank you, science and scientists), it isn't hard to imagine workable scenarios for creation in better accord with the process described by Moses. "And God said, 'Let the waters under the heavens be gathered together into one place, and let the dry land appear.' And it was so. God called the dry land Earth, and the waters that were gathered together he called Seas. And God saw that it was good" (Genesis 1:9–10).

Equipped with a better understanding of the earth and the revealed knowledge of Elohim, Moses' creation account is much more reasonable than many are willing to admit. Natural forces, guided by Elohim, may very easily have brought the world close to its current form in very quick fashion. Echoing the words of Jesus, "With man this is impossible, but with God all things are possible" (Matthew 19:26).

How Long for Life to Emerge upon the Earth?

Despite their contradictory timescales, both the scriptural and secular accounts follow roughly the same order of development of life. The earth took its shape and became stable enough to support life relatively quickly. Secularists say within the first billion years or so of the earth's formation, single-celled photosynthetic organisms became the first living creatures.[60] Moses recorded that as soon as the continents emerged, the earth *sprouted vegetation*: "And God said, 'Let the Earth sprout vegetation, plants yielding seed, and fruit trees bearing fruit in which is their seed, each according to its kind, on the Earth.' And it was so. The Earth brought forth vegetation, plants yielding seed according to their own kinds, and trees bearing fruit in which is their seed, each according to its kind. And God saw that it was good. And there was evening and there was morning, the third day" (Genesis 1:11–13).

Both the secular and scriptural models for the development of life on earth begin with green organisms. For our purposes, green living things include any creature that produces energy by processing carbon dioxide, primarily through the process of photosynthesis.[61] The green organisms—be they phytoplankton, algae, plants, or other green creatures—filled the atmosphere with the oxygen necessary for animal life to survive. These creatures still fill the atmosphere with oxygen needed to sustain life:

> The development of photosynthesis was possibly the single most important step in the evolution of life; it gave a primitive form of blue-green algae a practically unlimited source of energy. Photosynthesis involved

the absorption of sunlight by chlorophyll (in plants) to split water molecules into hydrogen and oxygen. The hydrogen combined with carbon dioxide, abundant in the early ocean and atmosphere, to form simple sugars and proteins, thereby liberating oxygen in the process. The growth of photosynthetic organisms was phenomenal ... Photosynthesis also dramatically increased the oxygen content of the ocean and atmosphere. The oxygen level jumped significantly.[62]

It would be hard to overstate how important the green life forms were in the preparation of earth for the establishment of animal life. Because they produce nature's biofuel (sugars) and by constantly replenishing the atmosphere with breathable oxygen, plants were necessary before animal life had a chance for survival.

Humanity is only beginning to understand the full importance of green organisms upon the earth. Emerging studies of the earth's oceans reveal the very broad basis for organic life that vegetation provides. NASA's Earth Observatory project explains the importance oft-ignored microscopic vegetation afloat in the ocean (phytoplankton) have had and continue to have on life: "Phytoplankton helped transform our atmosphere and pump it full of oxygen, paving the way for higher life forms. They still produce about half of the oxygen on Earth."[63]

Phytoplankton, too small to see with the naked eye, poorly-understood, and little-studied, is quite likely the all-important foundation of life on earth. If scientists compared the mass of plankton to all of the vegetation on land, plankton would far outweigh the photosynthesizers on land. Yet when was the last time most people thanked God for phytoplankton?

Here again, secular science may finally be catching up to what Moses described happening in Elohim's order of creation. According to Moses' account (and supported by current scientific thought), filling the world with vegetation was a necessary precursor to the rise of animal life. Darwin taught that through natural selection, early microbial life developed into all of today's life forms.[64] He also proposed that evolution began very early in the course of earth's history.[65] Although Darwin's mechanism for the development of life is very different from that of Moses, both accounts seem to agree that life developed on earth sooner than later.

There have been microscopic fossils discovered that show microbes present in some of the earth's very oldest rocks.[66] Could these fossils that litter the sea floor and have been found in the oldest bedrock support the idea of microbial vegetation present very near the beginning of time? Would it be unreasonable to expect that many of these early life forms have gone extinct due to the drastic climate change they may very well have had a hand in causing at the beginning?

As Moses told the story, Elohim didn't wait long for the earth to ripen so that life could sprout forth and develop. From a scriptural perspective, He created the earth to produce life. So why wait? Instead of a long evolutionary tale, Moses told the tale of a planet that was custom-made to support life. All of the necessary ingredients for plant life were on the surface of the earth by the third day—organic matter, water, and an environment stable enough for green things to grow. Plants immediately made use of these resources and readied the planet for higher creatures.

GEOLOGIC TIME AND CREATION

On this point, if the Genesis account is to be accepted, there must have been some form of spontaneous generation. This concept usually engenders resistance from the purely naturalistic and secular crowds. But then again, the purely naturalistic mentality has no room for the idea that Elohim could (and quite likely did) create mature elements on a young earth.

The notion of plants sprouting immediately fits well with what is known of Elohim's desires for the newly created planet. It also accords well with His ability to do things at a different pace than humanity can observe at work in the world today. Jesus repeatedly did the impossible during His earthly ministry. So for a person with a scriptural worldview, spontaneous generation of vegetation is not unreasonable. Considering Genesis within its own context, what would be unreasonable is to suggest that Elohim couldn't do this or that because we can't imagine this or that.

The fossil record indicates that the diversity of plants in the past was far more complex than what is observed today. Science hasn't yet fully considered how such a rapid cooling of earth and addition of green plants would have changed the chemical composition of the atmosphere. How such rapid changes on the surface of the earth could have led to global climate change hasn't been modeled, either. A vacillating climate could have easily allowed species that were at first marginally successful (and therefore absent or sparingly found in the fossil record) to become the dominant species observed in the world today.

The early earth, as Elohim created it, may very well have been dominated by life forms of Darwin's oft-mentioned Silurian Epoch.[67] Global warming and cooling could have changed the globe so much that the creatures most abundant at the beginning no longer survive today. The scriptural model of a planet that was initially full of life but is now plagued by extinctions (with no new species arising to take the place of fallen species) best explains what is observed today.

Elohim didn't need to wait for the earth to produce vegetation, because the power of His creative Word is such that mature plants could have been planted all over the earth. The creation itself began with Him creating everything out of nothing. When considering how these things may have come to be, it is wise to acknowledge—whether trying to explain origins from a scriptural or scientific perspective—that even our best hypotheses are based upon our current understanding of things and are liable to change. Genesis 1 is just a snapshot of earth's origins as recorded by Moses. It is accurate in what it says but limited to a tiny glimpse of what happened before any person was around to observe anything.

Musings regarding how these events happened is informed by current knowledge. Does Genesis provide a workable framework for creation? Yes. Is this interpretation reason to trump all other opinions or dismiss new findings pertinent to a better understanding of our origins? No.

Moses gave another snapshot of the first week of creation in Genesis 2 from more of an anthropic, or human-centered, perspective. At first, in Genesis 2, it appeared that there were no plants on the land. Later in that chapter, Adam was placed in a garden that was full of mature plants. Which is true? According to Moses (and Jesus, who quoted Moses to prove a point from time to time in the gospels), both are true as inspired words of Elohim.

These descriptions are not contradictory but rather are different perspectives of the same reality. This is no different than two eyewitnesses to a car accident giving equally accurate descriptions of a crash without necessarily highlighting all of the same details. In a courtroom, differing eyewitness accounts have more validity than identical testimonies.

Collusion usually means witnesses have been tampered with, which implies the truth is being covered up. This is also true of scriptural witnesses. Moses didn't try to make his two accounts of the creation sound identical, because he knew they were different perspectives of the same events. Those who wish to understand what he relates do well to acknowledge this and seek to understand Moses in light of his own context before dismissing his story in favor of another account because his story doesn't read like geology textbooks.

Secularists and creationists can agree that the processes whereby the earth gave rise to complex life required incomprehensible change. How this planet became hospitable to life hasn't yet been fully explained by science. Regardless of the model used to describe how the earth gave rise to human life, both secular and scriptural models start simple and become more complex with each successive age in roughly the same order.

The survival of every organism is dependent on conditions being ripe for the organism to survive *before* it can arrive on the scene. Take one necessary ingredient for an organism's survival out of the equation of life, and not only will an organism become extinct, but entire ecosystems also come tumbling down like a house of cards. The caring and careful Creator understood this and made everything ready to support life.

The existence of human beings is illustrative of this reality. Before people could arise, they needed to have things to eat, drink, and breathe. Before they could have things to eat, drink, and breathe, there had to be plant life producing food, shelter, and oxygen. Before plant life could produce food, shelter, and oxygen, the plants needed soil to put their roots into and water to drink. Before there was soil, there had to be organic material for the plants to build cells with—cells that could begin harvesting sunlight through the process of photosynthesis. This continues until the point where it isn't exactly clear what preceded what.

By the end of the third day, Elohim had created the universe, expanse, oceans, and dry land. The earth had matured into a roughly-finished state that was already hospitable to many forms of life. The earth was well-rounded and covered by seas and land masses that were filled with a number of green living things that produced their fruit for the procreation of their kinds and provided breathable air and food for the not-yet-created forms of animal life.

According to Moses, it was time for Elohim to begin filling the three distinct domains—the heavens, waters, and land—with a plethora of new creatures. The expanses and environments He created were ready to be filled with living beings. On the fourth day, He began filling creation with life by turning on the lights of His creation so that the light of His love could shine on the beings He intended to make.

The first, second, and third day furnished all of the raw ingredients for life and the environments where life would emerge. Examination of the fourth, fifth, and sixth days describes the life forms that filled each domain. According to Moses, all of this was done intentionally by Elohim, who put all of His creative wisdom and energy into the perfect place for the story of humanity to blossom.

LIGHTS IN THE EXPANSE
OF THE HEAVENS

The sun and celestial bodies are the shining stars of the fourth day. It is on this day that Moses described Elohim igniting the sun, illuminating the moon, and lighting the night sky with the starry host. He lit the heavens with no more difficulty than a twelve-year-old would have lighting the lights on a Christmas tree. Moses certainly had good religious reasons for listing the ignition of the sun on the fourth day. Secular science has also suggested very solid reasons to believe that the sun may have possibly begun burning after the formation of earth was already under way. "And God said, 'Let there be lights in the expanse of the heavens to separate the day from the night. And let them be for signs and for seasons, and for days and years, and let them be lights in the expanse of the heavens to give light upon the Earth.' And it was so. And God made the two great lights—the greater light to rule the day and the lesser light to rule the night—and the stars" (Genesis 1:14–16).

A tour through the fourth day will explore the religious and scientific implications of living on a planet that was well-formed before the sun started burning. Recent scientific insight reveals the wisdom behind Moses' arrangement. Had the earth not been well-formed and rotating when plants emerged, fatal doses of solar radiation would have most likely scorched a young earth and extinguished the development of any life on her surface. The arrangement of the Genesis account allowed for green living things to be pre-placed in order to harvest the sun's energy.

The fourth day is also an important turning point in the creation story, because Moses shifted his attention from Elohim's creation of the various realms (space, sky, seas, and dry land) to filling each with living creatures. The celestial bodies are detailed on the fourth day, bringing the night and day skies to their current appearance. Even when describing the creation of the heavenly bodies, Moses directed the reader's attention to the fact that they were created to serve useful purposes.

The fact that the heavenly bodies didn't make their appearances until the fourth day underlines the fact that the heavenly bodies are not to be worshipped. They are merely a part of creation. According to Moses, the Creator Elohim is the only one to be worshipped. The sun, moon, and stars are to be appreciated and respected as useful parts of creation but are not gods. But before discussing the theology of star creation on the fourth day, let us examine the secular evidence for believing that the sun was ignited after the formation of the earth was already under way.

WHICH CAME FIRST, THE SUN OR PLANET EARTH?

Thanks to innovations in technology and the advantage that modern telescopes have over primitive telescopes, humanity's understanding of the universe, including how stars form, has grown by leaps and bounds. In the decades since Edwin Hubble became the first person to observe galaxies outside of the Milky Way in 1924,[68] astronomers have been awakened to star-forming regions in space. New information based upon observations of areas where stars are still being born has birthed new theories regarding the origin of the sun.

Star formation is currently happening all around the cosmos. Under normal circumstances today, stars are formed when clouds of gas and dust condense under the weight of their own gravity until the internal density of the gaseous cloud reaches the point of critical mass to ignite a fusion reaction. Fusion is the engine that drives a star, producing the heat and light that astronomers observe and measure.

It has been proposed that after the big bang, the spreading matter and energy cooled and settled into areas where there was more matter, and therefore more gravity, to pull and hold everything together. This theory helps explain the variance in how much matter is found in dark places in space that are largely devoid of visible matter and the bright galaxies we observe that have much more visible matter than their surroundings. Where there was enough gravity, the density, pressure, and temperature increased to the point that stars began burning.

Star formation usually occurs in nebulae. There is enough raw hydrogen and pressure in many nebulae for fusion to begin and stars to ignite. Some nebulae are stellar nurseries—places where the conditions are ripe for many stars to be born and ignite.

Given the fact that star-forming regions still exist in space, there is the possibility that, at some point in the early history of the universe, many stars may have ignited at the same time. There was undoubtedly plenty of energy and matter swirling around in the primordial universe currently modeled by the big bang. If many regions of the expanding universe reached a state of critical mass in the same amount of time, there could have easily been a mass lighting of the starry host.

THE MOST IMPORTANT STAR AND PLANET PAIR IN THE UNIVERSE

One of the most important aspects of a stable planet (from a human perspective) would be proximity to a highly stable energy source. Life, as developed on the earth, needs stable temperatures and abundant energy. Stars—especially mid-sized, middle-aged stars—are the most likely candidates in the known universe to provide both.

Assuming that the sun was formed in the same way that stars are being formed and ignited today, secular science estimates that the sun is about 4.5 billion years old.[69] This calculation has been supported by a variety of measurements, including its composition, size, and temperature. At 4.5 billion years old, the sun is considered a middle-aged star.

Thankfully, this means the sun is far from dying. This is good news for the earth, because our sun is at the most stable point in a star's lifecycle. It has burned about half of its hydrogen, which means there is a long time until anyone needs to worry about the earth dying along with our sun (an estimated 4 to 5 billion years into the future, according to many leading scientists).[70]

If the data suggests that the sun is 4.5 billion years old, how could the composition of the sun and its suggested age (factors that appear to contradict the Genesis account) support Moses' narrative? It has already been suggested that Elohim desired to create the most hospitable environment for life. It would make sense for Elohim to create the sun in its current composition and state, because the middle of a star's life cycle is when it's most stable.

Those who prefer to think it is a lucky coincidence that the earth orbits a stable star are prone to imply that the sun is older than the earth. Insisting that the sun is older than earth is a tenuous proposition. Even though secular scientists currently disagree as to how solar systems are most likely to form,[71] they seem to be ready to agree that stars and their planets come into existence at about the same time.[72]

It appears that, under normal circumstances, the same force that causes a star's ignition (gravity) causes the matter that congregates around a star to flatten into a spinning disk of material that forms planets. If this is the case, one could argue that, depending on how quickly the matter collected into planet-sized clumps, a planet such as earth could have been relatively well-formed before its star ignited. If a star is born when fusion begins, then planets that had already begun to be formed would actually be older than their stars.

A side benefit to having a planet formed before its star ignited would be the removal of potentially fatal debris from the planet's orbit. When a planet is still forming, it needs material in order to add to its mass. Once formed, a collision with the very same debris that formed it could potentially destroy it.

Radiation and solar wind produced by a freshly ignited star would force much of the loose matter still swirling around a star out into space and away from planets that are large enough to be held in orbit by the star's gravity.[73] This wouldn't necessarily take all debris out of potentially dangerous orbits. However, it would give newly-formed planets a much greater chance of survival.

Granted, the secular models of planetary and solar formation rely on these forces taking billions of years to unfold. Proportionally speaking, the difference between three or four Genesis days is no greater than the difference between 5, 4.6, 4.5, or even 3.5 billion years (which is the amount of time it takes for the sun and the earth to take roughly their current shape, according to secular models). Whether one prefers the account of Moses or a favorite cosmologist, planet formation and star ignition appear to happen simultaneously, in the same order, and take roughly the same proportion of time.

EARTH'S PERFECT SHIELD FROM UNWANTED SOLAR INTERFERENCE

One fascinating feature of our planet that makes life possible that we are only beginning to understand is the earth's magnetic field. The magnetic field has proven useful to humanity ever since the earth's magnetism was discovered by the Chinese several thousand years ago.[74] But most people fail to recognize that not only is the earth's magnetism useful for navigation with a magnetic compass, but it is also quite possibly the shield earth needs to protect life.

Many people have personally had to deal with the unfortunate effects caused by too much exposure to radiation. Skin cancer is a growing threat to health and life, with more people being diagnosed every year. Whether the skin cancer is the result of too much exposure to natural or artificial UV light, this rising epidemic shows that too much radiation is a bad thing for living creatures.

It is radiation from the sun, stored as heat in our atmosphere and harvested by plants for food, that makes life on planet earth possible. But the sun constantly bombards our planet with more radiation than living creatures on the surface could handle. Thankfully, our magnetic field acts as a shield from most of the harmful radiation released by the sun.

Solar flares and solar winds are storms that carry streams of charged particles toward the earth, sometimes with damaging effects. [75] On March 13, 1989, the province of Quebec, Canada experienced a paralyzing power outage that was caused by interference from a solar flare that was so strong, it reached the earth's surface. Much of the power grid was down for many hours, because the electrical system was overloaded.[76] This episode was a warning that the same phenomenon that causes the beautiful aurora borealis (the northern and southern lights) can be deadly.

Society, which is increasingly dependent on extensive power grids and satellite-based communications, is vulnerable to inconvenient disruptions in service and widespread blackouts caused by solar storms. Astronauts in orbit far above the earth's surface are most vulnerable, because they are exposed to much more solar radiation than people on earth. Thankfully, almost all of the damage from solar events is mitigated by an extensive magnetic shield. Earth's magnetic shield may have even made life possible in the first place.

The magnetic shield extends beyond our atmosphere into space. Toward the sun, it is shaped like a perfect shield, deflecting most

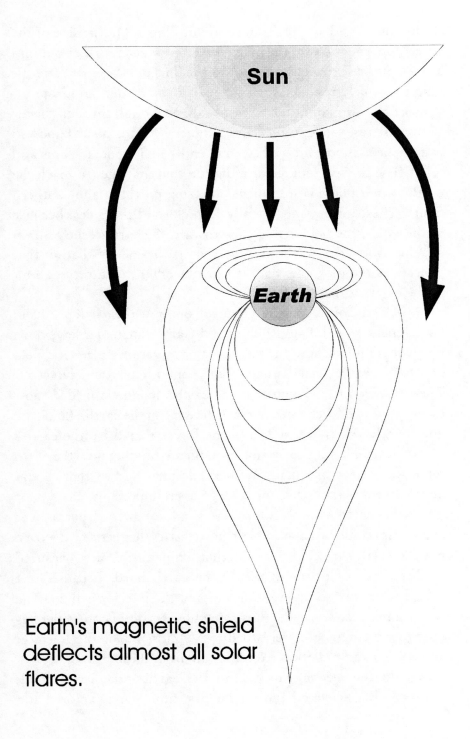

Earth's magnetic shield deflects almost all solar flares.

of the solar wind and flares around our planet. On the side of the earth opposite the sun, the magnetic field extends further out into space. Put these two geometries together around the earth, and the magnetic shield resembles the shape of an elongated raindrop.

Just as a drop of rain is perfectly shaped to fall through the air with least resistance, the earth's magnetic field is also shaped so as to deflect almost all of the sun's deadly ionized solar flares and wind. The tiny percentage of radiation that manages to reach the earth's atmosphere is seen in the amazing northern and southern lights. These auroras are usually seen close to the poles, because at the poles, the field bends back toward the earth. Like a drain sucking water down, the tiny percentage of solar radiation that penetrates the magnetic field is brought down toward the center of the earth near the poles.

Much study has gone into figuring out how the earth produces its magnetic shield. Paul Roberts and Gary Glatzmaier have done much to simulate how the earth may generate its magnetic field and have demonstrated some of the complex physics involved.[77] Their research has shown that the earth's magnetic field is most likely generated by charged currents flowing in the earth's fluid core and mantle. Their research into the forces that drive the earth's magnetic field have greatly amplified understanding how the earth retains such a strong magnetic field, despite the fact that earth's internal heat makes permanent magnetism impossible.

If the earth was a cold, rocky ball of metal, permanent magnetism could possibly explain how earth's magnetic field exists. But the earth isn't cold. Her internal temperatures are measured in thousands of degrees. Nor is the earth hard, because heat and pressure are so intense that most of the interior is fluid. The geodynamo theory has demonstrated how the fluid core generates enough of a magnetic field to direct almost all of the harmful ionized gas and radiation from the sun around the Eearth.

Could the mechanism behind the earth's magnetic shield, just recently discovered and for the first time being explored and explained by the scientific community, have been planned by Elohim from the beginning? We've already discussed the thin-shelled nature of our planet. A thin solid shell would allow for the most possible volume for a fluid core to produce as strong a magnetic field as possible. If this is one vital way the earth protects life, why must we assume that the earth couldn't have been created this way on purpose? [78]

USEFULNESS OF OUR PERFECT PARTNER PLANET—THE MOON

The magnetic field is very useful. So, too, is the moon. The moon serves as the perfect partner for planet earth. It would be next to impossible to imagine the earth without her moon. The moon brightens the night for very light-dependent humans. The moon makes the tides rise and fall. The moon marks the months of the year.

Despite the moon's usefulness, much of current scientific thought considers the moon a result of a cosmic accident. When the Apollo astronauts ascended to the surface of the moon, they collected rocks that were aged and analyzed after their return home. Scientists used the measurements and composition of the rocks to determine that the moon is nothing more than a conglomeration of stuff left over from a nearly fatal run-in between the earth and another protoplanet very early in the earth's development. [79]

Regardless of how you think the moon was formed, both secularists and creationists believe that the moon and the earth are roughly the same age. [80] Because the earth and moon are so close in age, it appears that they have been partner planets for life. Therefore, the moon is (and quite possibly has always been) the earth's perfect partner planet.

The full significance of the moon and how it affects life on the earth is still under much study. Animals are acutely aware of the moon. It doesn't take a genius to recognize the relationship between moon phases and animal behavior, especially its effect on the timing of breeding and spawning seasons. The rise and fall of the tides are essential to the survival of entire ecosystems where land meets sea. Forecasting the rise and fall of tides is vitally important to the success of fishermen, sailors, and many who depend on the oceans for their livelihoods.

One interesting aspect of the relationship between earth and her moon is that the barycenter of the earth-moon system lies within the earth.[81] This means that the tug of the moon's gravity is centered within the earth. This aspect of the earth-moon relationship profoundly affects the earth inside and out.

When a cook wants to stir ingredients in a bowl, he places his spoon inside the bowl, not outside. Could Elohim have figuratively done the same by placing the earth and moon so close to each other, perpetuating and driving many natural phenomena? Hopefully future scientific inquiry will explore deeper implications of the moon's close proximity to earth and reveal how truly important the moon is for many of the phenomena that make life possible on the earth.

It is easy to see how the moon affects life on the surface of the earth. But how the moon affects life on the surface is quite likely just the beginning of recognizing the full significance of the moon's location in close orbit around the earth. For instance, could the gravitational tug of the moon stir the fluid core of the earth, heating our planet from the inside while possibly fueling plate tectonics? Could the moon have a significant hand in driving seismic activity? In light of recent discoveries about how the earth generates her magnetic field, could the gravitational tug of the moon be propelling the geodynamo mechanism behind the earth's magnetism?

It is an exciting time for us to study the moon. New technology, radical theories, and ambitious scientists are pushing the envelope as they continue to unravel more and more mysteries about the earth. As understanding of the earth/moon relationship grows scientifically, so too will appreciation of the full importance of the moon for life on earth. "And God made the two great lights—the

greater light to rule the day and the lesser light to rule the night—
and the stars. And God set them in the expanse of the heavens to
give light on the Earth, to rule over the day and over the night, and
to separate the light from the darkness. And God saw that it was
good. And there was evening and there was morning, the fourth
day" (Genesis 1:16–19).

MOSES' INTENTIONAL MOVE AWAY FROM WORSHIP OF THE SUN AND MOON

At the time of Moses, it was common for both the sun and
moon to be worshipped. Moses intentionally contradicted many
of the themes of both Mesopotamian and Egyptian creation
narratives, distancing Israel from pagan worship of the heavenly
bodies. This offers one possible theological answer to the question
of why Moses would insert the sun and moon on the fourth day
of creation instead of earlier in the story.

Critics of a literal, faithful interpretation of the opening chapters
of Genesis love to pick on the fact that the sun was created on the
fourth day. They highlight that the Egyptians worshiped Ra, the
sun god, and suggest that the primary reason why the sun and
moon were relegated to the fourth day in Moses' creation account
was because Moses tried to distance his flock from the sun worship
that was prevalent in Egypt.[82]

Someone who believes that what the Bible says in Genesis 1 is
more than metaphor can reply by asking, "Why does a theological
motive need to be the *only* reason for Moses to place the ignition
of the sun and appearance of the moon on the fourth day?" If
the literal, physical order of creation accurately reflects the true
character of the spiritual realm, it may be possible that Elohim
designed it this way.

Could it not be possible that Elohim (who inspired Moses to
record an accurate description of His creative work) intended for
the literal order of creation to point humanity to Him, instead of
the heavenly bodies, as the true source of human life? If this is

the case, then one could easily square the actual order of creation with the theological aim of distancing the sun and moon from the beginning of all things. The physical realm could then be considered a literal, physical reflection of the spiritual realm and an accurate expression of Elohim's will.

The sun is vitally important to life on earth, as is the moon. Yet according to Moses, neither is absolutely necessary. Elohim was able to create light, which powers the biosystems of earth before (and therefore apart from) the sun. Elohim was the source of that light. The sun is nice and does much to sustain life on earth, but it is not necessary. It is worthy of respect and high regard as a wonderful gift from a benevolent Creator but does not deserve to be revered and worshipped.

As understanding of the heavenly bodies becomes more sophisticated, there seems to be a strong tendency to elevate the stars, sun, and moon to deity status. This is especially true among those who seek a purely naturalistic or scientific explanation of the origin of all things apart from Elohim. In order to draw the ire of those in the Christian community, some secularists even go so far as to refer to the stars with terms reserved by the church for Jesus Christ.[83]

Although this is not the time or place to delve into a deeper discussion about the implications of rationalizing Elohim out of existence, it is worth considering this concept. Could drawing conclusions about the existence (or lack thereof) of God based solely upon empirical evidence be a twenty-first-century return to worship the heavenly hosts? May secularists be guilty, in their rush to do away with Moses' Creator God, Elohim, of worshipping the stars in a new scientific way that fits the sensibilities of a secular, purely naturalistic, twenty-first-century mind?

If this is so, then the proponents of a purely scientific explanation of the universe should recognize the possibility that whether they like it or not, they may simply be worshipping a god of their own imagination and design. Wouldn't that blur the lines that some thought had been drawn between science and religion? Could it be that the lines once clearly drawn between science and faith may have actually been trespassed by those who most adamantly claim to keep science and religion separate and distinct?

The human race has always had great respect for the sun and moon. Sometimes, that healthy respect became unholy reverence. The moon, much like the sun, has often been an object of worship. One place where we find evidence of this worship is Qumran, overlooking the western shores of the Dead Sea in Palestine.

Qumran is significant for biblical scholarship due to the find of the Dead Sea scrolls. When visiting there, I learned that it has also long been a hotbed of moon worship. Qumran's namesake may be translated "two moons." The Dead Sea, below the height of Qumran, serves as a beautiful reflecting pool for the moon as it climbs the early evening sky.

It isn't hard to imagine why pagan moon-worshippers would choose to worship their deity in such a place. Excited by the appearance of two moons (one in the sky above, one on the sea below), they had a perfect place for their idolatrous worship. What a deal—worship two moons for the price of one!

Joshua wrote that before Moses died, he looked upon the Promised Land from Mount Nebo, east of the Jordan River.[84] Almost exactly across the Dead Sea from where Moses looked upon the Promised Land was Qumran, the place of moon worship. What an ironic place for Moses' life to end.

Moses' life's work was to bring God's people to a right relationship with Elohim through proper understanding of who their God was and who they were as His people. Moses spent his life teaching them that by the power of Elohim's Word, He made the earth, sun, and moon; created humanity; and redeemed His chosen people from slavery in Egypt. Elohim alone was their one true God. He alone was worthy of their worship. [85] Is it ironic or fitting that Moses' earthly life ended where worship of the moon may have begun? There are many layers to this intriguing tale.

The heavens complete, Moses' attention turned back to the earth. On the fifth day, Elohim filled the oceans and sky with living creatures. Do the creatures of sky and sea offer more reasons to believe that the natural world is the creative expression of Elohim's will? Or is Darwinian natural selection the only reasonable explanation for the myriad life forms found on planet earth?

SWARMS OF
LIVING CREATURES

"Swarming creatures" or "swarmers" are accurate ways to describe the most plentiful living beings on the earth. The oceans and skies are full of creatures that swarm, school, or flock. Yet most of these animals go unnoticed by us most of the time. Often, it isn't until a single swarmer gets zipped inside a tent while camping and one finds herself unable to sleep due to the persistent buzzing in her ear that these most plentiful living things are noticed.

Despite the fact that many consider swarmers pests and generally do their best to rid the world of them, earth is full of swarmers. Billions upon billions of swarming creatures and creeping things fill the earth. Throughout the seas and in the skies, there are creatures with fins or wings.

The fifth day was the day before the greatest day in Moses' creation account, because the sixth day was the day everything came together. In order for all things to come together, the earth was made ready for land animals by the creation of the swarmers:

> And God said, "Let the waters swarm with swarms of
> living creatures, and let birds fly above the Earth across

the expanse of the heavens." So God created the great
sea creatures and every living creature that moves, with
which the waters swarm, according to their kinds, and
every winged bird according to its kind. And God saw
that it was good. And God blessed them, saying, "Be
fruitful and multiply and fill the waters in the seas,
and let birds multiply on the Earth." And there was
evening and there was morning, the fifth day. (Genesis
1:20–23)

SWARMS OF SWARMERS

The term used by Moses for the swarmers of the fifth day most
likely included anything that crept or swam in the waters or flew
in the skies.[86] This description covers the vast majority of animal
species that live or ever have lived upon the earth. It would be
impossible to measure the full magnitude of biological life included
in this description, because the world is full of them. But there
are a few different ways to try to capture the vast scope of these
creatures.

One way to try to put the immensity of swarmers into perspective
is to count the number of species and figure out what percentage of
animal species are swarmers. Unfortunately, credible estimates for
the total number of species range from 3 to more than 100 million
species.[87] That's quite a wide array of credible estimates. Since it
is currently impossible to assemble a holistic listing of species, we
will have to trust the observations of a well-known and trusted
naturalist.

One researcher well-respected for his knowledge, particularly
of the insect kingdom, is the late J. B. S. Haldane. Even though he
was not known to be particularly fond of the church or notions
of a Creator, he described the incredibly diverse array of beetles
back in 1949 in the conclusion of his summary work, *What is
Life? The Layman's View of Nature* : "The Creator would appear
as endowed with a passion for stars, on the one hand, and for

beetles on the other, for the simple reason that there are nearly 300,000 species of beetle known, and perhaps more, as compared with somewhat less than 9,000 species of birds and a little over 10,000 species of mammals. Beetles are actually more numerous than the species of any other insect order. That kind of thing is characteristic of nature."[88] His is not an exhaustive listing of the total number of species, but his observation does illustrate the point that there are many more species of swarmers than of other animals—especially when one considers that swarmers include bugs, fish, birds, and all other winged or finned creatures.

Another way to attempt to put the immensity of swarmers in perspective is to consider how much of the earth is only suitable for creatures with fins or wings. Swarmers share the land areas with other creatures but have nearly exclusive rule of the skies and seas. The amount of space that is limited to the swarmers could provide a glimpse into how much life occupies that space.

We can compare livable space for swarmers and land animals by contrasting the volume of the oceans with the volume of space within 100 meters of the land (since terrestrial creatures are rather closely attached to the land they inhabit). The land area of earth is about 150 million kilometers^2. Dividing that area by ten (to give us the volume of space within one-tenth of a kilometer of land) reveals approximately 15 million kilometers^3 of habit suitable for non-swarming creatures.

Measurements by the National Oceanic and Atmospheric Administration estimate that the volume of the oceans is some 1.3 billion kilometers^3.[89] That means that the area reserved exclusively for swarmers to inhabit is nearly ninety times the space available for non-swarming creatures that are attached to land. It doesn't take a PhD in biology or ecology to recognize the probability that swarmers vastly outnumber other types of living creatures. This underscores their importance in the web of life. Every higher form of living creature is dependent upon them.

Four Forms of Swarmers

To put the massive diversity of swarmers that inhabit the earth into perspective, we will briefly touch on four major groups. Tiny sea creatures represent the most diverse, most significant, and possibly least understood of all animal life. Fish are next on the list, as they also inhabit the vast watery realm. Birds will be the third group, as they are found all over the world on both the sea and the land. Finally, insects—those bothersome creatures the Creator is rumored to have an odd affinity for—will be discussed.

The living creatures of the sea are so numerous and diverse that it's hard to imagine what *hasn't* been discovered yet. Here's one researcher's description of the diversity of sea life: "If a drop of seawater contains 160 species of bacteria (Curtis, Sloan and Scannell 202) and if a bucket contains hundreds of species of unicellular eukaryotes, the mind boggles at what the worldwide total might be."[90]

In other words, humanity has little understanding of the miniscule denizens of the ocean. Life in the ocean is so ill-understood that if you took a boat to many parts of the sea, filled a jar with water, took your jar back to a lab, and properly analyzed it, even today, you may be just as likely to discover a new species of organism as not.

The diversity of species yet to be discovered, especially if every cubic kilometer of ocean is filled with species uniquely adapted to fill each niche in the oceans, could be truly mind-boggling. Whether ocean species of microbes are as numerous as the imagination can dream up or a relatively small number of species inhabit vast stretches of ocean, the biological mass of such beings is bound to be immense.

Even in the deepest reaches of the oceans, life abounds. Deep-sea diving has only just begun, and divers routinely document creatures that have never been observed before. If, in deep-sea exploration, researchers only found one new species per square kilometer of ocean floor, that would leave some 10 million distinct species of creatures yet to be discovered.[91]

The most familiar of ocean swarmers are finned creatures. Fish, dolphins, whales, sharks, and every other finned or scaled creature that swims in the oceans are included within the swarmers of the fifth day. They are everywhere anyone looks in the waters. From the smallest fish fry to the great humpbacked whale (the largest living creature to ever inhabit the earth), the world's oceans, lakes, and streams are so fin-filled and diverse that the beauty and intricacy of marine habitats often isn't appreciated until they are threatened or destroyed. Sadly, this is because many people are so far removed from creation that they only appreciate finned creatures that can be found in a can—like tuna or sardines. The human race, which would like to imagine itself close to having the workings of the universe all figured out, can only marvel at the diversity found among finned creatures of the seas.

Birds were created right along with the finned sea creatures and are included in Moses' swarmers of the fifth day. Birds are found everywhere. There are species of birds found at nearly all altitudes and latitudes. Many survive migrations that take them thousands of miles and over vast stretches of ocean. The human race has yet to celebrate the hundredth anniversary of the first successful transatlantic flight; yet many bird species have successfully flown at least that far on migrations ever since they came into being.

Some bird species fly thousands of miles, including hundreds of miles over open ocean, to migrate. These include some of the smallest birds, such as the diminutive Ruby-Throated Hummingbird, which lives on nectar and could easily fit in an eight-year-old child's hand. Thousands of these tiny birds cross the Gulf of Mexico twice every year on migration. For such a tiny winged creature to survive such a journey is a feat much more impressive than crossing an ocean in an aircraft.

No discussion of the swarmers of the skies would be complete without bugs. It isn't inconceivable, given our limited knowledge of the insect world, that there could be more species of insects and creepy, crawling things than the number of species that have already been recorded. It is likely that people will never know exactly how many species of bugs there are. Even if researchers overturned every rock, log, and leaf and then sifted through every grain of sand and ounce of soil, they couldn't be certain they'd found them all.

The sheer volume of insects indicates that they have an important role to play in the story of creation. They are nature's janitorial crew as well as the primary source of protein for thousands of other animal species. Could their purpose be to fine-tune their environments so that ecosystems remain healthy and viable? Quite possibly the hardiest of all creatures, the most diverse and plentiful, they are yet another essential piece of the puzzle of life.

A Ruby-throated Hummingbird.

WHAT DOES IT MEAN TO BE ALIVE?

All of the living creatures of the fifth day were distinct from the plants created on the third day. But the question remains: what distinguishes plant life from animal life? From a purely naturalistic standpoint, the primary distinction between plants and animals is often seen in ability or inability to move: "The ability to move about under their own power is what essentially separates animals from plants, although some animals perform this function only in the larval stage and become sedentary or fixed to the seabed as adults. Mobility enabled animals to feed on plants and other animals, thus establishing new predator-prey relationships."[92] Moses noted more than just mobility distinguishing the living creatures of the fifth day from what was previously created.

It is interesting to note three of the distinguishing hallmarks of swarming creatures:

- They tend to be social. All of them congregate (or *swarm*, to use Moses' language) at least at some point in their lifetimes, many for their entire lifetimes.
- All of these creatures are designed to move about the face of the earth somehow, most by swimming or flying.
- They are consumers that must digest their food in order to survive. They are incapable of producing their own fuel like the green living things of the third day.

These three characteristics together—consuming their food, being social, and being able to move about—distinguished the fifth day's living things from everything else that was created before.

This brings up a fascinating discussion that may continue until the end of time: what is the essential difference between plants and animals? Is it the ability of an organism to produce its own fuel? Is it the ability to metabolize and move? Is it some manner of cognitive function? Is it some level of consciousness or self-awareness? Is it some measure of other human characteristics? Whatever the difference between plants and animals is, Moses made note, in his description of the fifth day, that these creatures were distinct from everything previously formed in creation.

For a student of the Scriptures and the person who seeks to know why anyone would choose to believe in Moses' account, it really helps to get into the original texts. These creatures have some measure of life, just as Elohim was alive. The line between Creator and creation was clearly drawn by Moses in the introductory verses of Genesis 1, but these creatures were more like their Creator than the raw material of creation, including the green living things from the third day.

These *living creatures* represent a huge step toward the creation of intelligent life. Scientists can debate what makes something alive. Regardless of how scientists classify organisms, Moses' distinction between the fifth day's living creatures and everything created prior to the fifth day indicates that something about the very nature of their beings makes them different from plant life. The two Hebrew terms together almost seem redundant, because they indicate having life in two different ways. They highlight for the reader that being truly alive entails some measure of living, not merely existing.

The creatures described on the fifth day were the first living creatures, according to Moses. Here again is the beginning of the Genesis account of the fifth day: "And God said, 'Let the waters swarm with swarms of *living creatures*, and let birds fly above the Earth across the expanse of the heavens.' So God created the great sea creatures and every *living creature* that moves" (Genesis 1:20–21a, emphasis added). It's hard to overstate the important leap this represents in the creation account.

Everything was building up to something. All of Elohim's creative work was coming close to its goal. Before the end, nothing would be turned into something, and that something would be alive!

The creatures of the fifth day enjoyed bodily lives that were granted to them in a fuller fashion than the plants and rocks. These creatures weren't just inanimate objects. Rocks, rivers, and even plants are inanimate. They exist, but they aren't alive in the same sense that animals are.

Elohim, on the fifth day, succeeded in bringing new life into the cosmos. Never before was anything besides Elohim truly alive. There was lots of physical stuff, even green things that metabolized via photosynthesis, but now the earth was full of biological life. This is an exciting juncture, because for the first time in the Genesis story, we can see life!

The advent of life is huge, because Elohim was crafting His creation to support life. A purely naturalistic, human-centered worldview sees life as one of an infinite number of possibilities that we just happen to be lucky enough to enjoy.[93] An Elohim-centered worldview sees everything as evidence of a Creator's deliberate plan coming to fruition. Like a master craftsman, He made everything the way it is so that people can live and enjoy life!

PYRAMID OF LIFE ALMOST COMPLETE

It is no secret that one of the most stable shapes for a building is that of a four-sided pyramid. The ancient Egyptians noted this and built their enduring monuments with such a design. A pyramid is rugged, durable, and can stand the test of time because of many properties, one of which is its balance.

If one compared the work of Elohim in Genesis 1 to a building project, a pyramid offers a good parallel. The foundation of the pyramid would be the light of the first day that provided a starting point and possibly all of the matter and energy needed to form everything else. On the second day, He separated the elemental earth from everything else. The third day defined the earth with distinct water and land masses and put into place all of the green living things that provide higher orders of creatures with their most basic needs—food, oxygen, shelter, and clean water. The fourth day set order to the operation of the earth by providing heavenly bodies for marking days, times, and seasons. With the addition of the first living creatures on the fifth day, the stage was set for the pyramid to be made complete with the creation of humanity as its capstone.

Scriptural Design for Creation's Development

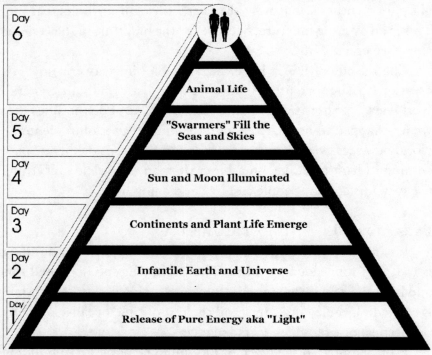

This order of creation—or framework or pattern, if you prefer—draws on Moses' repeated phrase, "and there was evening and there was morning." It seems that phrase is glanced over by many readers who are bored by its repetition. But the sentiment behind this phrase is vitally important to properly understand the nature of Elohim's design and carefully laid-out and executed plan.

Seeing Moses' account in the form of a pyramid is a helpful view of the Genesis story. Elohim worked toward the creation of humanity through many transitory steps. He started with the rudimentary raw materials and built up to the most complex creation—a human being. Each step was a further refining of what had existed before. He began with the most plentiful—and, consequently, most essential—life forms and worked his way up the food chain to the most complex. There is no sense of random development or blind guide, as all is engineered to support life.

Moses' model is completely opposite of Darwin's bottom-up process of development through natural selection. Both end with a world full of advanced life forms, but the means to the end are entirely different. Darwin noted the difference between his and Moses' description of how the world came to its current state while expressing his optimism that natural selection would replace creationism as the most accepted explanation for human origins: "Natural selection can act only by the preservation and accumulation of infinitesimally small inherited modifications, each profitable to the preserved being; and as modern geology has almost banished such views as the excavation of a great valley by a single diluvial wave, so will natural selection, if it be a true principle, banish the belief of the continued creation of new organic beings, or of any great and sudden modification of their structure."[94] Because the secular and scriptural models contradict each other, an upside-down pyramid better illustrates Darwin's path leading to the rise of complex organisms.

Evolutionary Model of Biological Development

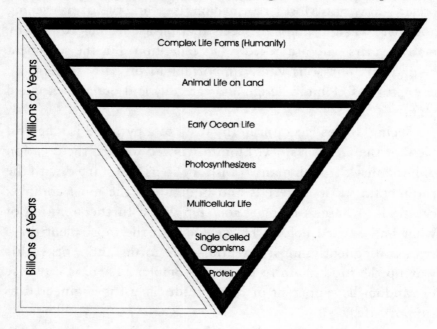

Darwin knew that his theory was opposed to the prevailing acceptance of creationism of his day. Was it folly or genius for a naturalist who lamented being able to properly classify species to suggest that he had discovered the mechanism that best describes how life has come to its present form? Darwin openly struggled with the difficulty common among the naturalists of his day (and even of our time)[95] to properly classify whether many organisms were distinct species or only variants.[96] Yet he had no problem promoting his own godless view of human origins over and above the scriptural description of how all things came to be.

His theory has received global acceptance and has been called by many "the best idea anyone ever had." He was a major innovator whose ideas have shifted the default view of origins away from Elohim toward a much more naturalistic (if not purely naturalistic) understanding of the world. He did nothing to change reality but radically altered how people perceive reality.

According to current models, there isn't really anything special about the life forms elevated by Moses' creation account. Bugs are just insects that happened to survive the gauntlet of life in order to procreate their species. They most certainly were not special acts of creation given the distinct honor of being among the first living creatures to inhabit the earth.

Is there anything special about life? Is there any reason beside blind, random mutation behind human origins? Or is the human race just the lucky winner of a cosmic jackpot?

On the sixth day, it will become clear that Moses proposed that people are much more than just a late addition to the circle of life. By living up to their full potential, human beings were designed to fulfill the purpose of all creation. They were created in the image of God to be like God, thus completing the work Elohim began when He brought the physical realm into existence.

IT WAS VERY GOOD

Before you can know who you are, it is necessary to know where you've come from. The study of origins is so intriguing and important because your origin informs you of who you are and where you are going. Once you know where you've come from, you will be much closer to knowing who you really are and may finally be able to reach your full potential.

Who you think you are (which is founded upon where you think you have come from) will always guide your actions, choices, and worldview. Although science has not yet been able to isolate self-consciousness and put it into a Petri dish (that's the "you" part of you or your spiritual essence), your understanding of yourself—especially your origin—is quite possibly the most important determining factor of your identity. Where you think you've come from will provide you with the default answer to every question you will ever ask about yourself and your life.

Unfortunately, many people today suffer from an identity crisis. I would venture to say that the conflicting claims between science and faith regarding our origins cause much of this conflict. Until we come to a correct understanding of where we've come from, how could we possibly know who we are? When we grope in darkness, unsure of who we are, much of life can be confusing at best or depressing at worst.

Your sense of identity is much more important in determining the outcome of your life than what happens to you, where you end up, who you marry, or anything else. Someone who has a wholesome understanding of self can endure anything and end up smelling like roses. Someone who has a poor understanding of self, no matter how successful he is or how great his life appears to be from the outside, can turn even the best circumstances toxic. In order to lead a truly meaningful and rewarding life, you must have a right knowledge of yourself.

Today, you get to listen to who you are in Elohim's eyes and according to Moses' description of creation! On the sixth day, humanity finally arrived on the scene (both literally and figuratively). Much time has been spent reading how Elohim set all of the pieces into place. Now, they will be put in motion, and creation will reach its fullest potential in a human being.

Moses built up to the creation of humanity as Elohim's masterpiece since the beginning of his account. Elohim took special care and concern in forming Adam from the earth and giving him his perfect mate. The creation began with Elohim. It was completed with people, who were created to be like Elohim in ways you and I can't even begin to imagine.

How great, wonderful, and amazing it is that Elohim created you to be like Him! Delving into the uniqueness of the sixth day will demonstrate some of the many ways creation was made complete with humanity. It will also become apparent that everything was made for the purpose of humanity to know the love of Elohim and be like Him. According to Moses, the only way that we will ever find our purpose fulfilled is in a perfect relationship with Elohim.

The goal of humanity is to find fulfillment in Elohim, not apart from Him. All too often, God is made out to be impotent at best or a sadistic tyrant at worst. But as Moses described Elohim, He is the greatest, created humanity to be like Him, and did nothing but set people up to reach their fullest potential in the perfect place for life.

Turning attention to human beings and the implications of Moses' description of creation, this chapter will take a decidedly theological turn. In order to weigh Moses' account properly, we must consider its implications for humanity without reference to the current controversies over our origins. At this point, such issues become distractions rather than fodder for a healthy dialogue.

Following is a look at the human race exclusively in light of Moses' description of the creation. Even if we are incapable of fully grasping all of the implications of what Moses described, an examination of Moses' theology will help readers grow in a understanding of humanity in light of Elohim's will. If Elohim truly is the Creator God, we will only ever achieve full potential by embracing that fact and learning from Elohim what His greatest hopes are for us.

THE EARTH BRINGS FORTH LIVING CREATURES

The sixth day began not with people, but with the other land creatures with which humanity shares the earth. Land animals were the final step in preparing the earth for human beings. "And God said, 'Let the Earth bring forth living creatures according to their kinds—livestock and creeping things and beasts of the Earth according to their kinds.' And it was so. And God made the beasts of the Earth according to their kinds and the livestock according to their kinds, and everything that creeps on the ground according to its kind. And God saw that it was good" (Genesis 1:24–25).

According to Moses, every land creature that has ever lived was created on the sixth day. "Beasts of the earth" include species that are still living today and many more that have long been extinct. Each species had its purpose to fulfill and its niche in the web of life.

Notice that all of the living creatures were created "according to their kinds." Each species was distinct from the others with a unique purpose to fulfill according to Elohim's plan. Many species may seem similar to each other. Some seem so similar that we may have trouble figuring out where one species begins and another ends. But Elohim knew them all and created each as a useful part of a diverse planet that was bursting with life.

God knew the differences between each life form and created each species unique for His purposes. No different than a maestro who uses many different notes to compose a breathtaking harmony, Elohim used millions of different creatures to write the book of life. Even the most complex and lovely music is written on one staff and composed of a few dozen notes. Multiply the notes millions of times to account for the number of species created to inhabit the pristine infant earth.

Can you imagine living in a world where all of the creatures of all time coexisted peacefully? Unlike the movie *Jurassic Park* (where everything seemed intent on eating everything else), living in the Garden of Eden would have been like living in a zoo filled with dinosaurs, lions, penguins, otters, and fish of all sorts. There would have also been untold species of birds, lizards, and all manner of creeping creatures. To top it all off, they all got along, ate plants, and did whatever Adam and Eve wanted. Such was the perfect world designed for humanity to inhabit.

How this planet could support all of those varying life forms at the same time is beyond imagination. If anything can be learned from what is observed in nature today, life was undoubtedly found everywhere. Life was so abundant, diverse, and wondrous that human beings wouldn't have been able to keep from praising God, who made earth and gave it to them to enjoy.

The land creatures, like the swarmers of the fifth day, were living creatures. They had physical bodies that needed to eat, breathe, drink, and sleep. They had some measure of intellect and were capable of making decisions, even if only instinctive ones. But they were only physically alive, not spiritually.

The land creatures were higher life forms than those previously created by virtue of having more characteristics in common with people, but they were still only physical creatures. If people are imagined to only be physical creatures, then the other land creatures and human beings seem to have almost every characteristic in common. Such an elevation of the land creatures (to basically the same status as humanity) is contrary to the design proposed by Moses. This reasoning elevates other land creatures by denying what made humans unique.

LET US MAKE MAN IN OUR IMAGE

With the land animals created, God only had one creature left to create, and that creature was you! It took special planning and preparation for humanity to be made just right. You can hear the special care Elohim took in forming human beings:

> Then God said, "Let us make man in our image, after our likeness. And let them have dominion over the fish of the sea and over the birds of the heavens and over the livestock and over all the Earth and over every creeping thing that creeps on the Earth."
> So God created man in his own image,
> in the image of God he created him;
> male and female he created them. (Genesis 1:26–27)

Never before in the story of creation did Elohim deliberate with Himself. According to Moses' description, He did just that before creating human beings.

In the introduction to Elohim at the beginning of Genesis, the one true God, *Elohim*, is plural, but the verb for *create* is singular. Here, a similar odd grammatical construction is used once again. This draws the reader's attention. This grammatical inconsistency is a literary clue that something is different about humans. Up to this point, Elohim simply spoke, and whatever He desired became what He wanted it to be. Much more attention went into the creation of people.

On the first day, Elohim wanted light, so He spoke, and it was. On the second day, Elohim wanted to set aside what would become earth and shield it with the expanse, so He spoke, and it was. On the third day, Elohim wanted the land and seas to be separated from each other and green living things to come forth, so He spoke, and it was. On the fourth day, Elohim wanted to light the day and night naturally, so He spoke, and the sun, moon, and stars appeared in the sky. On the fifth day, Elohim wanted to fill the seas and skies with living creatures that could move about, so He spoke, and it was. On the sixth day, Elohim wanted the earth to produce land creatures, so He spoke, and it was. But when it came time for people to be created, Elohim stepped back from the work He was doing. He deliberated upon it within Himself. He decided what human beings would be, how they would function, and who they could become. He considered what humans would do, and then He created them.

To the casual reader, the significance of Elohim's deliberation, planning, and careful creation of humanity may go unnoticed. But the special attention humanity received from Elohim at creation is essential to note if you are to fully understand humans in light of Elohim's creative work. It turns out that there is something unique to this particular creation. Not only is this creation a physical being, but it also shared in Elohim's spiritual nature!

Everything created thus far was only physical. The Creator, according to Genesis 1:2, was Spirit. Adam was created as a physical being with a spiritual soul. In humanity, the physical and the spiritual were joined. This spiritual nature made humanity unique in all creation. This is quite possibly the most significant aspect of being created in Elohim's image.

Once again, this all-important aspect of human beings—their spiritual nature—isn't something you can see in a microscope. You can't point to a region of the brain and say, "Yep, that's where it is!" This part of human nature is invisible; yet evidence of it is seen everywhere people worship, pray to a higher power, have feelings, care for others, feel some sense of right and wrong, or wonder if there's something more to this life than meets the eye.

Even though everything in life changes—friendships are formed and grow cold, bodies get older, friends and family pass away—there is a part of every person that never grows old. The spiritual nature, which is often referred to as the soul, never grows old. Your soul makes you the person you are. A human body without a soul is just a corpse. A human body with a soul is a living human being.

Every human being with a soul is alive. But even though you are physically alive, it is possible to not truly live life. Many people only survive. Elohim didn't create Adam and Eve to merely survive. He created them to thrive and live life to the fullest.

WHAT WAS IT LIKE TO BE IN ELOHIM'S IMAGE?

The image of God is something that humanity was given in Adam and Eve but has been lost for so long that we can only hope to begin to try to understand what it was like. God's indelible character was placed upon Adam, as evidenced by his spiritual nature. Martin Luther described Adam's natural attributes when he was created in Elohim's image:

> Both his inner and his outer sensations were all of the purest kind. His intellect was the clearest, his memory was the best, and his will was the most straightforward—all in the most beautiful tranquillity of mind, without any fear of death and without any anxiety. To these inner qualities came also those most beautiful and superb qualities of body and of all the limbs, qualities in which he surpassed all the remaining living creatures. I am fully convinced that before Adam's sin his eyes were so sharp and clear that they surpassed those of the lynx and eagle. He was stronger than the lions and the bears, whose strength is very great; and he handled them the way we handle puppies.[97]

According to this description, Adam's mental acumen, physical strength, and beauty surpassed anything anyone currently experiences.

Being perfectly in-tune with Elohim, perfectly at peace within ourselves, and coexisting harmoniously with the environment are no longer natural for us. Today, millions spend their lifetimes practicing meditation without ever achieving a state of nirvana (perfect peace of mind and harmony that is a goal of Indian religions including Hinduism and Buddhism). Millions of naturalists go to the great outdoors in search of peace and tranquility, but the creatures they wish to observe most often flee from them, while creatures they don't want to see often try to eat them alive. Even with much work and effort, humans cannot attain the harmony Adam experienced with nature within themselves or with God. What human beings now experience in this life is often closer to the opposite of the perfect peace Adam enjoyed without even trying.

The only person in the Scriptures besides Adam and Eve who wholly demonstrated what the image of God looks like was Jesus. Jesus showed by His selfless life and perfect obedience to His Father what a perfect life looks like. To most, He seemed to be just an ordinary guy. But when someone was in need and He leapt into action, He calmed storms, healed diseases, turned water into wine, made the blind see, made the lame walk, and even raised the dead! Such is the power of the one conceived in the image of God and perfect in His obedience to His heavenly Father.

Read again how deliberate Elohim was in creating humanity in His image: "So God created man in his own image, in the image of God he created him; male and female he created them" (Genesis 1:27).

Some could make a big deal about the tripartite form of this verse. Is there a correlation between the triune nature of God and the human having a mind, body, and soul? Such a tripartite division of the human being could make sense as a reflection of the Triune God. Just as one cannot divide the Trinity without losing the Godhead, you cannot separate a person's body, mind, or soul without killing a person. This metaphor is helpful in describing humanity at creation but doesn't capture the entire essence of being created in Elohim's image.

There is also something to be said for giving human beings a will to decide what they would do, who they would be, and how they would exercise true freedom. Just as Elohim had a free will as God, Adam was also given the right and ability to decide for himself. Humanity's freedom allowed for growth.

A free will also made a true and reciprocal love possible. Perfect love was the basis of Adam and Eve's relationship with their Creator, Elohim. His love was not forced on them; it was freely shared. A truly free will was a vitally important aspect of human nature, because it opened the door to a relationship that was based on love and trust. Everything would work well so long as Adam and Eve loved their Creator, each other, and the creation they shared.

According to Moses, humans were elevated far above every other creature. Humanity is far superior to other living beings, even heavenly bodies, because they were the only beings created in Elohim's image with a spiritual nature and truly free will.[98] Having a spiritual nature gave humanity a connection with God that no other creature enjoyed. A truly free will was also unique among the earthly creatures. Bearing God's image separated humans from every other creature in ways that can't be downplayed if you are to truly appreciate your place in Elohim's creation.

CREATED IN THE LIKENESS OF ELOHIM

Not only did Adam and Eve bear Elohim's image, but they were also perfectly like God. To many, being like Elohim is considered synonymous with bearing His image, but this is not the case. Bearing the image implies resembling the Creator perfectly (again, in ways that can no longer be fully fathomed). Likeness indicated how well Adam and Eve resembled their Creator.

Adam and Eve were, by their very nature, perfectly like God. Because God is perfect, Adam and Eve were perfect. As the perfect creation of a perfect Creator living in a perfect world, Adam and Eve enjoyed life as it was meant to be—perfect.

Everything existed in perfect relationship, because people were just like their Creator in how they thought, acted, and believed. Their intellect was such that they automatically understood things as they were. When they cared for each other, living creatures, and the earth, their actions mimicked the one who made them. Their hearts were filled with an innocent, childlike faith, because they knew Elohim was their loving heavenly Father and never doubted His love and care.

Created in the image and likeness of Elohim, people had unlimited potential. They had unlimited capacity for growth and unlimited faith. They enjoyed eternal life. That's the way Elohim made it.

BLESSED TO GROW AND RULE THE WORLD

Created in Elohim's image and in His likeness, humans were blessed to grow and rule over the natural realm Elohim had created:

> And God blessed them. And God said to them, "Be fruitful and multiply and fill the Earth and subdue it, and have dominion over the fish of the sea and over the birds of the heavens and over every living thing that moves on the Earth." And God said, "Behold, I have given you every plant yielding seed that is on the face of all the Earth, and every tree with seed in its fruit. You shall have them for food. And to every beast of the Earth and to every bird of the heavens and to everything that creeps on the Earth, everything that has the breath of life, I have given every green plant for food." And it was so. (Genesis 1:28–30)

According to Moses, people had much to do in creation. Elohim gave them charge to govern and care for all that He had made. That was quite some task, but absent death, it isn't hard to imagine that it wouldn't have taken the human race long to spread over the face of the earth and subdue it.

There is unlimited potential, within this blessing, for people to fulfill! They were perfect, but they weren't a finished product. Yes, they bore Elohim's image and likeness, but He wasn't finished with them when He created them. Rather, their perfection came in the form of innocence. One could think of their innocence as childlike innocence.[99] They may or may not have been created physically mature, but emotionally, spiritually, and intellectually, they were childlike.

Evidence of humanity's potential for growth is still observed, because it is natural for people to seek improvement in every area of life. This is a trait retained from Adam and Eve. Elohim created them to grow in knowledge through learning. He created them to grow in their relationship with Him by faith. He created them to grow closer to each other through love. He gave them the opportunity to use their bodies and thereby mature physically. He taught them His will and way so that they could grow in their faith and reliance upon Him.

When Elohim gave Adam and Eve a free will to decide for themselves how they would grow and eventually reach the full measure of their human potential, He took the training wheels off in a world that provided a safe environment for them to learn in. By exercising their will and choosing what was right, Adam, Eve, and their descendants were to prove their God-likeness. They were to exercise purity and righteousness forever as physical and spiritual beings. No other creature was given such a high calling with a foot in both the physical and spiritual realms of existence.

IT WAS PERFECTLY GOOD!

Everything in the physical realm was created for the purpose of revealing Elohim's love to human beings. They were equipped with minds, bodies, souls, emotions, and wills to comprehend and appreciate Elohim. Human beings were created to be the primary beneficiaries of Elohim's undeserved, unending, and unconditional love.

The literary clue Moses employed to make this point is heard in the final verse of Genesis 1: "And God saw everything that he had made, and behold, it was very good. And there was evening and there was morning, the sixth day" (Genesis 1:31). Each previous day in the creation account ended with Elohim overlooking what He had made and stating that it was good. Midway through the sixth day, after creating the land animals, He also said that what had been made was good. After creating people, God looked over what He had made and declared it to be "very good!"

The Hebrew words rendered "very good" could be translated as "greatly good," "exceedingly good," "much good," "perfectly good," "super good," or "forcefully good," but none of these fully convey the extent of the original Hebrew. Were I to choose one rendering for brevity's sake, it would be "perfectly good" (which gets the point across but may not be the most literal translation) or "greatly good" (which is more literal but not as powerful).

According to the story of origins as described by Moses, you are the reason everything that has been made was made! Your purpose is to know the unconditional love of God, grow in that love forever, and never tire of exercising your freedom by being a blessing to God, other people, and all of creation.

People were created as the principle beneficiaries of an eternally benevolent Creator God. When Elohim created humanity in His image and made them in His likeness, He shared all of creation and His very self with us. We were created to be like God and know Him as He truly is. We are created to enjoy a perfect relationship with Him, each other, and our world.

God's Design for Creation

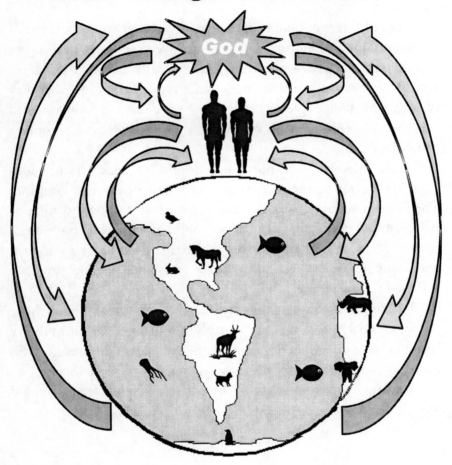

Everything in perfect harmony according to God's will. "God is Love" (1 John 4:16).

People also enjoyed the freedom that came from having the free will to make decisions. They were to learn from their decisions and grow in a right understanding of self, each other, their environment, and the Creator. Their heavenly Father gave them the keys to His car, so to speak, so that they could go out, explore, and learn what it meant to be like God. With freedom came unlimited potential to be great and do great things for God, each other, and other creatures.

Not only were human beings created, but they were also blessed exponentially by Elohim. His blessing gave them growth in every aspect of their lives—physically, numerically through children, socially, emotionally, spiritually, intellectually, and any other way it is possible for people to grow. They were created to grow until they became fully mature by exercising their will and becoming fully like God.

When Elohim gave humanity dominion over all that was created, He made them co-rulers with Him over His creation. That's a lot of responsibility, and it's a great calling. So long as Adam and Eve lived within God's will, they would have been perfect servants and rulers over the earth. Everything existed in perfection, and they were given the responsibility to make sure that it stayed that way.

To think that humanity is the reason God created everything is too wonderful for anyone to fully appreciate. Adam and Eve couldn't have imagined doing anything but praise Elohim for who He is, what He did for them, who they were, and the perfect relationship they enjoyed with Him. They were perfectly created and perfectly blessed to enjoy a perfect lot in life.

THE SEVENTH DAY

Moses' description of creation ended with Elohim resting on the seventh day. The Sabbath day is still honored by many observant Jews and some Christians as a day of worship and rest. Whether or not you are religious, it is also the reason most people in the West don't work on Saturday.

With everything complete, Elohim enjoyed the beauty and harmony of His perfect creation: "Thus the heavens and the Earth were finished, and all the host of them. And on the seventh day God finished his work that he had done, and he rested on the seventh day from all his work that he had done. So God blessed the seventh day and made it holy, because on it God rested from all his work that he had done in creation" (Genesis 2:1–3). The creation account didn't end when creating activity was done. It ended when Elohim intentionally paused after His creation was formed.

Why Elohim rested is a matter of debate. It has been noted that Elohim took a break so that human beings would have a divine permission slip to take time to relax and enjoy life instead of laboring all the time. It appears that Elohim may have known what He was doing in offering an opportunity for rest when one reads of a newly recognized phenomenon—people apparently working themselves to death.

In Japan, a potent poisonous cocktail of workful restlessness has been brewed. A deadly mix of cultural expectation and economic pressures on workers has led thousands to work themselves to sickness or death. *Karoshi* is the term coined for those who die at work of heart or brain conditions that have little to no explanation other than that the employee worked too much.[100] People need rest, so Elohim gave a divine pattern for workers to follow when He took a break on the seventh day. Is there more to this divine rest than simply the fact that God rested so that we have His permission to?

Is it possible that the divine rest was a transitional period between the time of Elohim's dramatic creative activity and the beginning of natural time, which we now perceive as the *normal* passage of time? If everything slowed down when Elohim finished His creative activity on the seventh day, it isn't difficult to imagine why natural processes seem to work so slowly today when compared to the rapid pace of development described in Moses' creation account.

Regardless of your view of how long creation took, it appears that everything in the material realm sprung into existence from nothing very quickly. Scientists are busy trying to explain how this may have conceivably happened. But until humanity is freed from the constraints of time, there will be some measure of wonder and marvel at how everything came to be.

Leaving further investigation into the workings of the material realm to the scientists for now, it is time to turn attention back to the Scriptures in search for a reasonable understanding of the brokenness now observed in people, their relationships, and the world at large. Knowing no purely natural cause for why everything ends up broken, did Moses provide a reasonable cause for why everything seems so messed up?

What Moses described in the beginning—a perfect planet filled with life and perfect people who loved each other unconditionally and trusted their Creator wholeheartedly absent death and suffering—is *not* what people experience today. Is there a rational explanation of the inconsistency between what was created then and what is experienced now? The Scriptures reveal how Elohim's perfect creation full of life unraveled to the point that it is now plagued by death.

TAKING A CLOSER LOOK AT THE GARDEN OF EDEN

Genesis 2 offers a close-up view of the place where Elohim placed people to live. Here, Moses offered another perspective to help show how perfect Adam and Eve's home was for fostering their growth and development. It began,

> These are the generations of the heavens and the earth when they were created, in the day that the LORD God made the earth and the heavens. When no bush of the field was yet in the land and no small plant of the field had yet sprung up—for the LORD God had not caused it to rain on the land, and there was no man to work the ground, and a mist was going up from the land and was watering the whole face of the ground—then the LORD God formed the man of dust from the ground and *breathed into his nostrils the breath of life, and the man became a living creature.* And the LORD God planted a garden in Eden, in the east, and there he put the man whom he had formed. And out of the ground the LORD God made to spring up every tree that is pleasant to the sight and good for food. The tree of life was in the midst of the garden, and the tree of the knowledge of good and evil. (Genesis 2:4–9, emphasis added)

This portion of Moses' description reiterates that Adam's life came from Elohim's life, which was breathed into Adam at his creation.

A human being minus a soul is just a physical body or corpse. A human being with a spiritual soul is connected to Elohim in ways that can't be fully appreciated. Connected to the Creator through a perfectly loving relationship, a human being is truly alive—both physically and spiritually.

People were created in Elohim's image and likeness. In order to grow in His likeness, they were given a free will to exercise their likeness to God. The spiritual soul is one aspect of God's image. Having a truly free will was another very important part of bearing His image.

Part of living life (as opposed to merely physically surviving) is being able to make decisions, learn from them, and grow. Adam and Eve were given the ability to decide for themselves how they would or wouldn't exercise their likeness to God. Their lives flowed from the one who created them to be like Him and continued so long as they were like Him.

So long as Adam and Eve lived like Him, everything continued to work perfectly, just as it was designed. They were created to live in love toward each other and with perfect faith in Elohim. They were formed to mimic Elohim as caretakers of all He had made. So long as they lived up to their calling, they—and all of creation—were blessed to live forever.

THE TWO TREES IN THE MIDDLE OF THE GARDEN

In order for Adam and Eve to be able to exercise their freedom, Elohim placed two trees in the center of the garden. These trees were both good, because they afforded Adam and Eve the opportunity to exercise their likeness to God by choosing what was right, thus exercising their own righteousness. The fruit of the Tree of Life was the right choice. So long as they ate from it, they would live forever in righteousness. Attached to the fruit of the Tree of the Knowledge of Good and Evil was the consequence of death.

If Adam and Eve were to have the real choice between good and evil, there had to be options. The two trees in the middle of the garden represented their options: "The LORD God took the man and put him in the garden of Eden to work it and keep it. And the LORD God commanded the man, saying, 'You may surely eat of every tree of the garden, but of the tree of the knowledge of good and evil you shall not eat, for in the day that you eat of it you shall surely die'" (Genesis 2:15–17). The first option (God's way) was to eat from the Tree of Life and thereby live in perfect love, faith, and innocence forever. The second option was offered them so that they could live life their way instead of God's if they so chose.

God *lovingly* attached the curse of death to the Tree of the Knowledge of Good and Evil so that if Adam and Eve chose evil instead of good, He could *mercifully* end their suffering. There are worse things than physically dying. Being spiritually dead and thus separated from the Creator's love forever is the worst possible thing that could happen to a human being who is created to live forever in a harmonious relationship with Elohim. Had Elohim allowed Adam and Eve's physical lives to continue forever after turning away from Him and becoming spiritually dead, their lives would have quickly become hell on earth.

Many close the book and stop reading here, because they can't imagine that death could ever be thought of as a good, loving, merciful thing with which Elohim would threaten humanity. This is where Elohim is treated as the bad guy by many who blame Him for all of the suffering and evil observed in the world today. In my pastoral experience, many have told me that what they experienced in life was worse than death. Before addressing concerns such as what could be worse than death, we must take a step back and consider a world without both of those trees in the garden. In other words, we must consider the artificiality of a world with no real choices and therefore no true freedom.

If Elohim didn't place both trees in the garden and thereby deprived Adam and Eve of the ability to respond to His love by choosing to be like Him, one could argue that He was more of a bully or monster, because He forced them to love Him by depriving them of any other option. Humanly speaking, love that is manipulative or coerced is called abuse. Love that is physically forced upon someone else is rape, which is universally considered among the worst crimes against another person. Even though many don't understand or appreciate the consequence attached to the Tree of the Knowledge of Good and Evil, Elohim gave people a real choice so that they could have a real love- and trust-based relationship with Him that was neither coerced nor forced.

Elohim didn't create robots. He did not fill the earth with inanimate objects that may very well have revealed His glory without being appreciated by anyone besides Elohim. He made people with hearts and souls, flesh and blood, minds and emotions. He created physical, spiritual, social, intellectual people. He also equipped them with wills so that they could appreciate Him and His creation while growing in His image and likeness.

In order to be Elohim's free people who could fully appreciate Him, Adam and Eve were given their minds, bodies, souls, emotions, senses, and truly free wills. In other words, He gave them everything they needed to support their bodily and spiritual life. The two trees in the middle of the garden were essential parts of His plan to enable humanity to live, grow, and mature by exercising their inherent likeness to God in faith forever!

GOD RESTED, BUT SOMEONE WASN'T SLEEPING

As Moses told the story, Adam and Eve weren't the only beings who were given truly free wills. They were the only beings created with a physical and spiritual nature, but there were other spiritual beings who were given the choice to live in a right relationship with Elohim or try to live their own way instead. The angels were spiritual beings who are given the ability to choose for themselves whether they would serve and honor Elohim or turn away from God by serving themselves.

The serpent in Genesis 3 represents the fallen angel Satan, who deceived Adam and Eve. Satan wanted to be God, but since he couldn't be God, he was intent to become his own god by serving himself and inciting as many other beings as possible to do the same:

> Now the serpent was more crafty than any other beast of the field that the LORD God had made. He said to the woman, "Did God actually say, 'You shall not eat of any tree in the garden'?" And the woman said to the serpent, "We may eat of the fruit of the trees in the garden, but God said, 'You shall not eat of the fruit of the tree that is in the midst of the garden, neither shall you touch it, lest you die.'" But the serpent said to the woman, "You will not surely die. For God knows that when you eat of it your eyes will be opened, and you will be like God, knowing good and evil." (Genesis 3:1–5)

If Satan couldn't dethrone Elohim, why not try to be the god of human beings? They were the ones who were created in Elohim's image, bore His likeness, and were given dominion over the earth. If he couldn't defeat Elohim, conquering humanity would be the next greatest prize.

Satan knew exactly what he was doing when he tempted Adam and Eve. He didn't blatantly contradict God's Word at first. He merely questioned it, hoping that doubt would chip away at the perfect faith Eve had in her Creator. If he could get her to question, then doubt, then deny, and finally disobey Elohim, he knew that God's perfect creation would be broken. In control of Adam and Eve, he would become lord over Elohim's creation.

When Elohim gave Adam and Eve dominion and authority over the earth, He withheld nothing from their control. If they fell into sin, all of the material realm would follow them into their servitude of Satan and be broken. Satan wanted to ruin creation by bringing death into it and wanted Adam and Eve to worship Him instead of Elohim. If they chose Satan's way over Elohim's way, the perfect relationships, peace, and harmony that had been created would be shattered.

One may ask, "If Adam and Eve were created perfect, how could they have possibly sinned?" One is correct in asserting that they were perfect. But there are different ways you can view their perfection.

One way to view their perfection is as childlike innocence. Irenaeus (a second-century church father, many of whose works have been preserved by the church) described Adam and Eve as being perfectly innocent with unlimited potential for growth. They were created to exercise their childlike innocence in perfect righteousness.

Living in faith toward Elohim and love toward each other, they would have grown until their innocence was perfected by a faith that was fulfilled by their obedience. This was how they were to become fully like God. Their righteousness would be proven as they learned what it was like to live and be perfectly like their Creator.[101]

Satan was also created in righteousness and given the opportunity to be like Elohim by using his gifts and abilities in service to God and others. Instead, he turned inward to serve himself. He denied his Creator and became his own god.

Satan wanted Adam and Eve to do the same. If he, as a spiritual being, brought godlessness into the spiritual realm, how great an accomplishment it would be for him to get Adam and Eve to bring godlessness into the material realm. "So when the woman saw that the tree was good for food, and that it was a delight to the eyes, and that the tree was to be desired to make one wise, she took of its fruit and ate, and she also gave some to her husband who was with her, and he ate. Then the eyes of both were opened, and they knew that they were naked. And they sewed fig leaves together and made themselves loincloths" (Genesis 3:6–7).

Adam and Eve became wise by choosing what was wrong instead of right. Awakened to the knowledge of good and evil by their willful disobedience to Elohim, they realized that they were now out of a right relationship with God. They had unwittingly opposed God by defying His will.

When they tasted the fruit, Adam and Eve immediately knew they had done wrong. Guilt and shame were born. For the first time in their lives, they felt naked and ashamed of who they were and what they had done. In their attempt to become like God, they chose death for themselves instead of life. As God's chosen caretakers of creation, their corruption brought the brokenness of death into the world.

They tried to cover their sin, but nothing they could do would undo the choice they made. I'm pretty sure that when God saw them sporting their tailor-made, fig leaf loincloths, their sin was made even more obvious by their shallow attempt to cover it up. Like a little child may try to cover spilled milk with a napkin instead of cleaning it up, they tried to hide what they did but only made their sin more apparent. They didn't know what to do. They were brokenhearted and afraid of the one who had only ever shown them love and care.

Satan had, by his lies, won Adam and Eve over to his side. Little did they know that the freedom they once enjoyed—the ability to choose for themselves whom they would serve and what they would do—was lost. They had become Satan's slaves by offering up their wills to do his will. This broke the perfect relationship they had with Elohim.

It was a cruel bait-and-switch; yet it worked perfectly as designed. Satan may never be God, but by deceiving Adam and Eve, he became their god. His lies would become their native tongue. His self-serving intent would become the base motive for everything humans would do. They would begin to try to assemble a view of the world with themselves, instead of Elohim, at the center.

PERFECT RELATIONSHIP WITH ELOHIM
AND EACH OTHER BROKEN

Elohim created Adam and Eve in His image to be like Him so that everything would work the way it was designed. Life would have been unending. Everyone would have gotten along. In short, everything would have existed in perfect harmony with Elohim at the center.

When Adam and Eve decided that they were going to do things their way instead of Elohim's way, they ordered their lives with themselves at the center. This helps explain why people are naturally selfish or self-centered. When human beings decide to put their own wants, needs, and ambitions above the needs of others, relationships are broken, people get hurt, and suffering is caused.

Even young children display humanity's inherently selfish attitude. How many ten-year-old students have had to suffer the disapproving gaze of a teacher for coming to class unprepared after one of their friends "borrowed" something they needed for class from their locker without asking? You don't have to teach children to search their neighbors' lockers at school for ink pens when they've forgotten theirs. But you do have to teach them to share what they have. We don't put valuables in lockers because people naturally respect others' possessions. We guard our belongings with lock and key because people don't naturally respect our property.

Such is the fallen state of human nature. This is quite the opposite of Elohim's nature. He made and did everything for the sake of others. It now seems normal for people to put themselves first.

Man's Choice for Creation

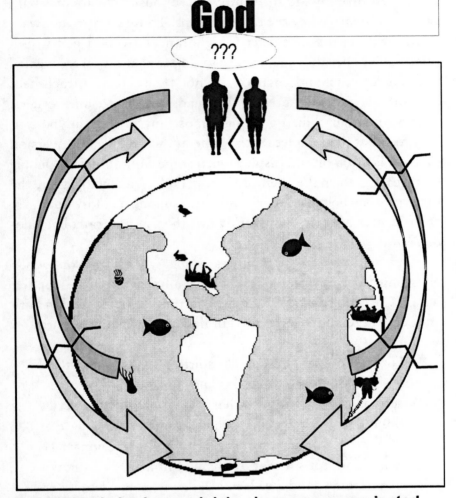

**Everything is broken and dying because man rejected
God's will in favor of his own way.**

One need not ascribe to the biblical worldview to see the
brokenness of the world. Buddhists hold that at the root of all
suffering and evil are the three poisons of ignorance, attachment,
and aversion. These are three base manifestations of the self-
centered orientation of human beings. [102]

A scriptural interpretation of what happened when humanity decided to turn inward for fulfillment, opposite of Elohim's will, can be summarized by the three poisons. Those who are unaware of the true nature of existence (ignorance) are destined to put others down, because people have forgotten that they were created to serve Elohim and each other, not themselves. Attachment (an unholy desire or greed) also leads people to hurt others, because many can justify doing almost anything to anybody if they feel that their choices satisfy one of their felt needs. Aversion (hatred) is often on full display when something threatens people or threatens to make them uncomfortable. Taken together, the three poisons help us understand why (so long as individuals are at the center of their own worldview) the self naturally becomes one's god.

This self-centered brokenness is felt within the soul when wrestling with our consciences. St. Paul described the conflict within Christians who are spiritually attuned to trust God in faith and serve others in love yet are faithless and selfish by nature:

> For we know that the law is spiritual, but I am of the flesh, sold under sin. For I do not understand my own actions. For I do not do what I want, but I do the very thing I hate. Now if I do what I do not want, I agree with the law, that it is good. So now it is no longer I who do it, but sin that dwells within me. For I know that nothing good dwells in me, that is, in my flesh. For I have the desire to do what is right, but not the ability to carry it out. For I do not do the good I want, but the evil I do not want is what I keep on doing. Now if I do what I do not want, it is no longer I who do it, but sin that dwells within me. So I find it to be a law that when I want to do right, evil lies close at hand. For I delight in the law of God, in my inner being, but I see in my members another law waging war against

the law of my mind and making me captive to the law of sin that dwells in my members. Wretched man that I am! Who will deliver me from this body of death? (Romans 7:14–24)

Human beings are stuck with a selfish nature, because when Adam turned from being selfless (which flowed from being created in Elohim's image), the image he chose for himself was the opposite.

How much damage Satan was able to accomplish when he led Adam and Eve into rebellion is incalculable. When humanity's relationship with the Creator was broken, humans immediately felt that brokenness within themselves. Evidence of their brokenness is felt within us and seen at work in others, because all humans are now selfish by nature. Their brokenness was also immediately transferred to all of creation, because when they fell to sin, all of creation fell.

What had been a perfect place where all creatures got along and cared for each other quickly disintegrated into a selfish free-for-all. Instead of lions lying next to the lambs, they began eating them. Rather than seeing creation as providing for all of their needs, people began to feel threatened by it. In short, love and trust turned into hatred and fear. People began trying to understand reality with themselves at the center in order to make some sense of life apart from God.

HUMANITY REMAKES GOD IN ITS IMAGE

After the fall, Adam and Eve quickly put all of the trust they had in their Creator into themselves. Unbeknown to them, by trusting in themselves and their own ability to figure things out, they were actually putting their trust in the one who opened their minds to godless possibilities. Satan had dominion over them, and they had unwittingly bound themselves to his lordship for the rest of their natural lives. Godless possibilities quickly turned out to be anti-God probabilities.

Elohim became viewed by His creatures as the monster. Never mind the fact that He had created them and that it was only His love for them that kept them from being swept out of existence forever. What had been love for humanity's Creator became hate. What had been faith and trust was replaced by disbelief and fear. What was created in perfect harmony was in conflict.

Adam and Eve, crushed by their guilt and shame, *needed* a new worldview that would somehow let them off of the hook for their crimes, even if it was nothing more than a fabrication. It was a lie that plunged them into the darkness of death. Why not perpetuate the lie by convincing themselves that the root of their problems was Elohim? This way, they could try to become the solution to their lives' problems, since they only trusted themselves.

The human race has inherited Adam and Eve's disdain for the ways of Elohim and complete lack of trust in Him. This is why it makes sense for people to try to solve life's big questions apart from Elohim. When people refuse to look to Him for an answer to life's problems, their lives are often spent turning to anything and everything but Him to make life make sense.

This is seen when people who are limited by the natural forces at work in the world tend to imagine ways God *couldn't* have possibly created everything that exists. It is normal for people to imagine that *if* He exists, He *must* be limited by the same natural phenomena as humanity. Because all anyone naturally knows is what he or she can see with his or her physical eyes, people imagine that God either doesn't exist at all or if He does exist, He must be handcuffed (as we are) by natural laws. If He does exist and isn't limited, it's normal to think of Him as being distantly removed from the natural world.

Instead of listening to God's Word and accepting who He says He is, it has become natural to imagine that God is nothing more than an exaggerated version of a person. People prefer to worship gods of their own design instead of the one who has designed and created them. Ancient pagan gods were often exaggerations of human traits. Religions of the ancient Near East usually associated their gods with natural phenomena and worshipped gods of strength, fertility, war, and the like. The Romans and Greeks worshipped gods who lived "soap-opera" lives.

This sort of religion makes sense to humans, not because these gods reflect reality, but because they are like us. By default, people now worship gods created by the human imagination. Such is a counterfeit attempt by fallen humanity to find fulfillment by way of a relationship with fictional gods. It is ironic that people who were created to be like God would rather worship gods imagined to be like people!

DEATH BECOMES VIEWED AS THE SOURCE OF LIFE

In the most recent machinations of human ponderings of origins apart from Elohim, death has taken the lead as the most reasonable contributor to the development of life. The current recipe for life is a combination of death on a cosmic scale (supernovae and the like) and death along biological lines (Darwinian natural selection and evolution). This explanation of life makes perfect sense from a purely naturalistic mindset.

People are surrounded by death in every arena of life. But could it be that the death we observe in life is actually evidence of a brokenness that has crept into all of creation? Doesn't it make more sense to think of death as an unnatural interruption of life instead of the giver of life?

Before dealing with the implications of purely secular explanations of our origins, it needs to be reiterated that science is a wonderful thing. The pursuit of natural knowledge has provided humanity with a much more holistic understanding of the human body, the world, and the universe. The wealth of riches yet to be uncovered in scientific inquiry should be mined in a quest for a deeper understanding of the material realm. This should be done while limiting implications of scientific discoveries to the physical realm.

Testable, observational science that admits that it is bound within time, just as scientific observers are, is pure science. The use of theories based solely on observations of the physical realm to try to answer questions of a spiritual nature is not science. When this happens, science can become our religion.

If natural forces are viewed as the source of life, people run the risk of worshipping those forces as gods. Many may unintentionally worship such gods of human imagination and design. Excluding Elohim from theories of human origins on the basis of scientific principle in the name of science and then using science to deny Elohim perverts what science seeks—an unbiased, objective truth that can be proven by experiment.

In reading many current authorities on humanity's best understanding of cosmology and quantum mechanics, one finds it in *en vogue* to employ Occam's razor when the question of God comes up. The line of thought is that any notion of the supernatural complicates scientific inquiry because supernatural causes or forces are untestable and unverifiable. In principle, excluding a variable you can't account for or control in an experiment is good science.

When the same scientist who uses Occam's razor to limit experiment to observable, physical phenomena makes a case, based upon his science, to argue against the existence of a spiritual God, he has misled himself. Such science denies God by mixing pure observational science with the scientist's godless worldview. A spiritual God can't be observed in physical experimentation, but that doesn't mean He couldn't possibly exist. In the end, such pseudoscience promotes an anti-God religion.

If one appeals only to the naturalistic mind when trying to determine why humanity came into being, here are some of the postulates that make more sense than Elohim creating the universe:

- You have just won the cosmic lottery! You just happen to be reflecting upon your origins because, mathematically speaking, in an infinite universe with infinite possibilities, your assemblage of organic matter just happened to come together so that you are alive today. As a matter of fact, it is quite possible that there are an infinite number of beings identical to you in other pockets of the seemingly infinite universe.[103]

- Something inevitably springs from nothing, because nothing is inherently unstable; therefore, we were bound to be here sooner or later. [104]
- Aliens seeded infant earth with life.
- That amoeba (a shapeless, single-celled life form) floating in the gutter have the potential to evolve into another being identical to you in about 4 billion years.

In these schemes, random chance, infinitesimally small possibilities that are bound to happen sometime somewhere in an infinite universe, or even alien life (which we have no real proof exists) are considered more credible explanations for life than Elohim. Isn't that what should be expected of a species that declared its independence from God and has ever since been desperately searching for anything else (inevitably, something else in the natural realm) to be its God?

How many times has it been stated throughout this discussion that God can't be observed in a telescope or microscope, because He is, by His nature, spiritual? Physical creatures are only able to observe the physical realm with their physical eyes. This means that human beings will never directly observe Elohim unless He decides to make Himself known.

How Is Humanity to Know Elohim if He Can't Be Physically Observed?

Were Elohim to reveal Himself somehow, shouldn't it be expected that He would manifest Himself in a way that was perfectly clear? Wouldn't it also make sense that most of humanity, blinded by a purely naturalistic mindset, would miss it? Of those who perceived God's revelation of Himself, wouldn't it also make sense that most people would probably reject Him, because humans have become selfish beings who are now, by nature, opposed to Elohim's selfless nature? This becomes even more likely when one recognizes that humanity has hardened itself against its Creator since the beginning.

If the Word of Elohim (which was the agent of creation according to the Scriptures) is still working in creation, humanity should appeal to the Word (instead of telescopes, microscopes, particle accelerators, and meager imaginations) to answer the spiritual questions regarding human origins. Many scientists claim to probe the mind of God by way of their experiments without ever acknowledging Elohim as God. It has become acceptable to deny Elohim based upon scientific principle. But to deny Elohim without ever listening to His Word makes no more sense than condemning science as anti-God before evaluating scientific theories.

Science, based solely on natural knowledge, has its place in answering questions about the physical realm. The Scriptures, based on a revealed knowledge of God, are best suited to answer questions about the spiritual realm. The Scriptures don't oppose the sciences. Instead, they lead humanity to a deeper understanding of life by revealing the connection of all things physical and spiritual. This is most especially true if, in the Scriptures, the Word that was spoken at the beginning is still being spoken into creation.

Scientists don't grow in their awareness of the physical realm by running sloppy experiments. Similarly, no one will grow in a deeper awareness of the spiritual realm by picking up the Scriptures just long enough to throw them away. More implications of a scriptural worldview will be explored in the final chapter. But before going there, it needs to be reiterated that neither Elohim nor the Scriptures is anti-science. Science can become anti-God if it becomes viewed as the only source of truth. But acknowledgement of Elohim as Creator in no way denies science.

If the God of the Scriptures is the Creator of everything and the Word brought everything into existence, then to come to a correct understanding of existence, the Scriptures and science must complement each other. Both describe different aspects of a complex reality that human beings, as spiritual and physical beings, occupy. This means that despite the difficulties and apparent contradictions between the Scriptures and science, there must be some way for everything to come together.

According to the Scriptures, the only way everything makes sense is in the person of Jesus Christ, the place where the spiritual and the physical, humanity and the divine, intersect. The apostle John taught that Jesus is the very Word of God: "In the beginning was the Word, and the Word was with God, and the Word was God. He was in the beginning with God. All things were made through him, and without him was not any thing made that was made. In him was life, and the life was the light of men ... And the Word became flesh and dwelt among us, and we have seen his glory, glory as of the only Son from the Father, full of grace and truth" (John 1:1–4, 14). In this passage, John made it very clear that in Jesus, God literally entered His creation by becoming a human being.

John began his gospel at the beginning of time to make it crystal clear that Jesus is much more than just a late addition to the story of Elohim's relationship with humanity. Genesis isn't the only book of the Bible that begins at the very beginning of time. John's gospel also begins, "In the beginning" so that Elohim's work begun in creation isn't divorced from His work being completed in Christ.

The seventh day of this discussion has shown how, through sin and disobedience, death entered the world. When Jesus was conceived, the very Author of Life was born to breathe Elohim's life back into creation. As God and as a human, Jesus revealed Elohim's plan for His creation by fulfilling it Himself. He has given humanity hope by destroying death with His own death. By rising to new life on the eighth day, Jesus reopened the kingdom of God to fallen humanity and brought life and immortality to light.[105]

THE EIGHTH DAY

In the perfection of Eden, after giving Adam and Eve truly free wills to decide for themselves whom they would serve and who would be their God, Elohim told them very clearly what the consequence of a poor choice would be. He couldn't have made it any clearer or simpler. Eat from the Tree of Life, and live. Eat from the Tree of the Knowledge of Good and Evil, and die.

This was Elohim's way of giving Adam and Eve freedom and the opportunity to exercise the righteousness they had by virtue of being created in His image and likeness. Love, peace, and joy abounded so long as they chose to be like their Creator. As soon as they chose otherwise, everything succumbed to the brokenness of death.

When Adam and Eve decided to try to live life their own way, they brought sin and death into the world. This wasn't a small dilemma for them or their Creator. Their choice threatened to forever destroy the work Elohim had done in creation. If something wasn't done, all would have been lost.

Elohim faced a problem. He had created the universe, earth, Adam, and Eve to exist forever in perfect harmony. Dissonance and discord became natural as soon as His will was broken. *Everything* succumbed to death.

Adam and Eve couldn't fix their problem. Elohim didn't offer them an easy way out. Because He is perfect, righteous, and holy, He couldn't just wink at their sin to make it go away. The consequence for sin decreed by God in the beginning, death, had to be carried out, or else He would prove to be imperfect, unjust, and unholy.

What God says must always be done. By the power of His Word, nothingness, disorder, and darkness were replaced by an orderly universe filled with the light of life. If Elohim's creation was to ever go back to the way it was before the brokenness of death overtook creation, Elohim would have to do something even more glorious than bringing everything into existence in the first place.

For most, death seems like a hateful reality for God to inflict upon humanity. This is not so when one recognizes that God is able to use even death to draw people back to Himself. Through Jesus' death, forgiveness and salvation came. Through physical death, God frees His saints from sin, suffering, and death by the power of the resurrection.

The most basic message of the cross—the Creator God taking sin upon Himself and dying for His creation—may not make sense to self-centered, sinful human beings at first. But when one comes to know Elohim as He revealed Himself in the Scriptures (a perfectly loving, selfless God who did everything for His creation), this foreign concept begins to make sense. Elohim's love, a self-sacrificing love, only makes sense when one begins to come to terms with the revealed knowledge of God in the Scriptures. It is alien to the natural disposition of human beings.

This is why Jesus Christ is God's revelation of Himself *par excellence*. His life, death, and resurrection show that Elohim's love for people knows no bounds. By His life, death, and resurrection, God the Son, "The Word became flesh and dwelt among us" (John 1:14), has opened the kingdom of God to all people. The church celebrates this new life, born of death and fulfilled in the resurrection, on the figurative eighth day.

The Significance of the Eighth Day Today

Ever since the time of the apostles, the eighth day has been set aside by Christians as the day of worship. The Sabbath, the Old Testament day of worship and rest, was fulfilled by Christ's rest in the tomb. The seventh day now marks the symbolic end of the old order of things—a creation that was corrupted by evil and death. Sunday, the metaphorical eighth day, became the day of worship for early Christians, because it was on the first day of the week (the eighth day) that the Son of God stepped victoriously from His tomb.

Luther described the significance of the eighth day:

> In an allegorical sense the eighth day signifies the future life; for Christ rested in the sepulcher on the Sabbath, that is, during the entire seventh day, but rose again on the day which follows the Sabbath, which is the eighth day and the beginning of a new week, and after it no other day is counted. For through His death Christ brought to a close the weeks of time and on the eighth day entered into a different kind of life, in which days are no longer counted but there is one eternal day without the alternations of night.
>
> This has been thought out wisely, learnedly, and piously, namely, that the eighth day is the eternal day. For the rising Christ is no longer subject to days, months, weeks, or any number of days; He is in a new and eternal life.[106]

Life lived in light of the eighth day is new life lived in faith. Christians share in the new life of Christ through faith that is founded on the revealed knowledge of God.

Both the prophet Isaiah and St. Paul connect the work of Christ explicitly to what Elohim began in creation: "But now thus says the LORD, he who created you, O Jacob, he who formed you, O Israel:

'Fear not, for I have redeemed you; I have called you by name, you are mine'" (Isaiah 43:1). "Therefore, if anyone is in Christ, he is a new creation. The old has passed away; behold, the new has come. All this is from God, who through Christ reconciled us to himself and gave us the ministry of reconciliation" (2 Corinthians 5:17–18a).

The work began at the moment of creation, when Elohim created light in the darkness and gave life to His creation, seemed to grow dark when evil and death corrupted creation. It was the son of God, Adam, who brought death into existence. It is the Son of God, Jesus, who breathed Elohim's life back into the dead and dying world.[107]

In light of Christ, the Word made flesh, Elohim's light shines even more gloriously than it did at creation. Elohim, who first formed a perfect creation, has redeemed His fallen creation and made holy that which once was lost. All of God's work, from creation to Christ and until Christ returns in glory, can now be cast in light of the seven-day creation and metaphorical eighth day.

LOOKING AT LIFE IN LIGHT OF THE EIGHTH DAY

Christ and His resurrection provide the the lens through which Christians interpret their reality, because Jesus was how Elohim fully revealed Himself to humanity. He is the foundation upon which Christian faith and thought is built. Life takes on a whole new meaning when the mind is open to God's work in Jesus Christ. In Him, the physical and spiritual realms are connected in a way that the faithful can attain the most complete knowledge of reality.

The belief in Jesus Christ as Savior and Lord is not contrary to the study of the natural world through science, even if it is founded upon the revealed knowledge of God in the Scriptures. A scriptural understanding of human origins and the role of Christ as Savior in no way undermines science. Rather, faith in Christ equips the mind with a framework that sees God at work in all things: "The heavens declare the glory of God, and the sky above proclaims his handiwork. Day to day pours out speech, and night to night reveals knowledge" (Psalm 19:1–2). "For what can be known about God is plain to them, because God has shown it to them. For his invisible attributes, namely, his eternal power and divine nature, have been clearly perceived, ever since the creation of the world, in the things that have been made. So they are without excuse" (Romans 1:19–20).

Elohim may be hidden from the physical eye, but He has left indications of His presence throughout creation for humanity to explore and ponder. Knowing that Elohim has created everything to be studied and explored so that we can grow in the knowledge of God through a more intimate knowledge of His creation gives scientists freedom to learn as much as they can in their quest for knowledge.

CHRIST, THE WISDOM OF GOD, FROM BEFORE THE BEGINNING

In Elohim, there is no disconnect between thoughts, Word, and actions, because God is one. There is perfect harmony within the Godhead, and there is perfect alignment within God. It may be superficial to compare divine thoughts, Word, and creative action to human thoughts, words, and deeds, but it can be helpful for coming to a better understanding of how all things in both the material and spiritual realm come together in Christ.

Human beings, creatures of a fallen nature, are prone to exhibit the dissonance of the soul created by sin, because their lives reveal an ongoing conflict between thoughts, words, and actions. Part of the human condition is an inherent inability to say exactly what was meant or to do exactly what was intended. This is because human beings no longer reflect the perfect image of Elohim impressed upon Adam at his creation.[108]

When Elohim created the universe, creation was produced by the perfect alignment of divine thought, Word, and deed. This alignment of purpose was described by the writer of Proverbs. He described wisdom personified as the divine thought (God's plan and will) that brought everything into existence:

> The LORD possessed me at the beginning of his work,
>   the first of his acts of old.
> Ages ago I was set up,
>   at the first, before the beginning of the earth.
> When there were no depths I was brought forth,
>   when there were no springs abounding with water.
> Before the mountains had been shaped,
>   before the hills, I was brought forth,
> before he had made the earth with its fields,
>   or the first of the dust of the world.
> When he established the heavens, I was there;
>   when he drew a circle on the face of the deep,
> when he made firm the skies above,
>   when he established the fountains of the deep,
> when he assigned to the sea its limit,
>   so that the waters might not transgress his command,
> when he marked out the foundations of the earth,
>   then I was beside him, like a master workman,
> and I was daily his delight,
>   rejoicing before him always,
> rejoicing in his inhabited world
>   and delighting in the children of man. (Proverbs 8:22–31)

According to this passage, divine wisdom was the blueprint, creative force, and coworker with Elohim at the creation of the material realm.

This passage describes a beautiful relationship between God and wisdom—a working partnership that joyously brought everything into existence. Some have suggested this passage is simply a metaphorical reflection upon divine wisdom—a poetic personification of wisdom and her virtues. But if this wisdom is thought of as the very same creative Word from John 1, Jesus is wisdom. In this sense, it is wisdom personified, the Word made flesh in Jesus Christ, who created humanity and has dwelt among us.

According to this depiction, at creation, God delighted in Christ and in humanity. The fall into sin and death threatened to undo what God had done. But even sin and death can't break Elohim's relationship with creation, because God doesn't change. He didn't have to change, because in Christ, God still delights in us.

The proverb continues,

And now, O sons, listen to me:
   blessed are those who keep my ways.
Hear instruction and be wise,
   and do not neglect it.
Blessed is the one who listens to me,
   watching daily at my gates,
   waiting beside my doors.
For whoever finds me finds life
   and obtains favor from the LORD,
but he who fails to find me injures himself;
   all who hate me love death. (Proverbs 8:32–36)

In the beginning, at creation, Elohim brought light and life into existence. According to His own plan and for His own good pleasure, He made everything. Christ has now come into creation to bring the light of life, which had been obscured by the darkness of death, back into creation.

He fulfilled the plan of creation not by setting it aside or destroying what had been created. Instead, He redeemed all of it. He now uses physical death as the means to free humanity from eternal, spiritual death through the power of His resurrection. Such was the will of Elohim from the beginning.

God, His plan, His purpose, His power, and ultimately, His love have all been revealed in Jesus Christ. This is why Christians stubbornly hold to Christ and His Word as the final authority in all matters of life and faith. "In him was life, and the life was the light of men. The light shines in the darkness, and the darkness has not overcome it" (John 1:4–5).

FAITH *AND* (NOT *OR*) SCIENCE

Once one understands the difference between the revealed knowledge of God from the Scriptures and natural knowledge that is studied in the sciences, the conflict between faith and science is greatly diminished. It takes both kinds of learning to come to a unified understanding of the physical and spiritual realms. Sacrificing one for the sake of the other leaves people (who were created with physical bodies and spiritual souls) missing all-important pieces of life's puzzle.

To suggest that Elohim or Christians are anti-science would be the same as suggesting that Henry Ford was anti-automobile or that Thomas Edison was anti-lightbulb. Many Christians may feel threatened by scientific development, and church leaders have sometimes stood in the way of scientific progress. But Elohim shouldn't be held accountable for those misunderstandings any more than a parent should be condemned for a crime committed by his or her son or daughter.

Many secular scientists may firmly believe that any faith in God undermines pure, reasonable scientific inquiry. But to imagine that God or the Scriptures are completely irrelevant because Moses' Genesis account doesn't read like a physics textbook is unreasonable. Genesis still stands as an unaltered, inspired account of the beginning that can't be disproven by science after 3,500 years.

Compare the longevity of the Genesis account to the track record of secular science's best guess at the estimated age of the universe (which has grown from 1.5 billion years to almost 14 billion years in less than a century). Christians have good reason for holding on to their inspired account, because it need not change. Sure, secular science may shed light on how all things may have come to be, but secular theory alters our view of the beginning without actually changing the beginning. Christian scientists, acknowledging the limitations of the human mind and the constraints time puts on humanity's best efforts, hold to the inspired account while trying to figure out how everything may have come to be.

It has proven difficult for many secular, scientifically-minded and Christ-centered people to engage in a meaningful dialogue about origins because of entirely different foundations of thought. One foundation is based exclusively upon natural knowledge, and the other is based upon a revealed knowledge of Elohim in the Scriptures. However, a meaningful discussion of human origins theories (and consequently, the implications of those theories) is not impossible, because there are many who have no problem looking at reality in light of both science and the Scriptures. These people have the greatest chance of coming to the most complete understanding of human origins.

Faith sees Elohim at work in creation and views science as a means through which people can grow in understanding of the material realm. Faith doesn't fear scientific exploration or the implications of scientific theory, because the Scriptures provide an inspired framework within which science operates. The Scriptures are the framework used by the faithful to sort out the best of scientific theory and apply it to daily life.

Faith doesn't dismiss or deny science, but it does temper science by cautioning against overstepping the bounds of human speculation. Scientists may propose possibilities for how all things came to be, but time has proven that even the most brilliant scientific theories are subject to revision, because new information inevitably arises to challenge previously accepted notions of scientific fact. Real progress in the sciences will only continue if a new generation of scientists arise who are able to hold two apparently contradictory views of reality in tension long enough to genuinely test the validity of both. Otherwise, scientific fads will be accepted as facts, and popularly accepted wisdom may quickly devolve into foolishness.

Christ-centered scientists are not a threat to scientific inquiry and thought. They may very well be best equipped to make headway in every scientific field, because they are competent and confident enough to challenge currently held assumptions that may in the very near future be shown to be dead wrong. Courage to explore flows from a humble opinion of self and unwavering confidence in the One who already knows the answers to even the most difficult questions. Growth will be a blessed result of searching for those answers in faith.

Although many will disagree, I believe that when it comes to the faith versus science debate, it is possible to appreciate and learn from both. This is only possible if we are careful to discern when and where science and religion venture into foreign territory reserved for the other. It takes humility, a willingness to learn, and openness to exploration in order to grow, but aren't these attributes of a wholesome view of the world that makes learning so exciting and fun? Aren't these virtues, along with learning how to live within our limitations, part of being human?

Some have recently suggested that the faith versus science debate will wind down over the next generation or so and that one side or the other will be victorious. The tension between the secular and scriptural accounts of humanity's origin will most likely remain until the end of time. It is through wrestling with the tension between the divine account of creation and our best current understanding of the material realm that humanity grows into a deeper understanding of origins.

Since conflict was thrust upon creation, conflict has been used by Elohim to bring His people to a deeper understanding of existence. He did not create the conflict, but He has used conflict to teach His people about the futility of searching for life's meaning apart from Him. He has also taught humanity the depth of His love by becoming the greatest casualty of the conflict we caused by dying on the cross.

Thus, Elohim has revealed Himself as the beginning, middle, and end. He is the Creator, Redeemer, and Sanctifier of all that exists. Only in Him and in light of His plan will humanity see the light of life. Apart from Him are only darkness and death.

There is growth, development, and hope in the midst of conflict, and so conflict between the faith and scientific communities about our origins will most likely remain until the end. The faithful should not fear such conflict but rather embrace it as God's means for humanity to grow into an ever deeper understanding of existence. Is the struggle to come to terms with human origins frustrating? Yes. Is this struggle within self and with others who hold very differing views damning? No—at least, not so long as Elohim is God and individuals recognize their place in His plan.

According to the Scriptures, real growth is only possible so long as Christ remains the focus of meditation on such mysteries. "Again Jesus spoke to them, saying, 'I am the light of the world. Whoever follows me will not walk in darkness, but will have the light of life'" (John 8:12). "Jesus said to him, 'I am the way, and the truth, and the life. No one comes to the Father except through me. If you had known me, you would have known my Father also. From now on you do know him and have seen him'" (John 14:6–7). "Now faith is the assurance of things hoped for, the conviction of things not seen ... By faith we understand that the universe was created by the word of God, so that what is seen was not made out of things that are visible" (Hebrews 11:1, 3).

What a blessing it would be to see this and future generations embrace a Christ-centered view of the sciences in our search for the ultimate truth about human origins. Only with Christ at the center will we as individuals, and collectively as a species, come to the most complete possible explanation of the mystery of mysteries.

ACKNOWLEDGMENTS

There are many who have helped bring *On Our Origins* into existence. Without the love, encouragement, and support of many, this project would have never been completed. These are the ones whom I owe tremendous gratitude for helping me to create something out of nothing.

To my wife, Wendi, and our children—you are my greatest earthly blessing, and I count every day spent living this life with you as a great treasure.

To my church family at Redeemer and the Redeemer Foundation—this work is as much your work as it is mine, because it has flowed out of our ministry together. In our time together, you have taught me more than I have taught you.

To four individuals who worked patiently with me through many drafts, Raymond B. Williams, Rev. Philip Hale, Bill Ferguson Jr. and Dan Davis—I am indebted to you for your wisdom, theological aptitude, creativity and guidance.

To all who have had more faith in me than I have in myself—I am grateful.

Most importantly, there would be no one to thank or anything to be thankful for had the Author of Life not given His own life up so that we can enjoy this life and the next with Him as Lord and Savior. To Him be all the glory, honor, praise, and thanksgiving from this time forth and forevermore.

WORKS CITED

The Holy Bible, English Standard Version. Wheaton, IL: Crossway, 2001.

Bauer, Walter. *A Greek-English Lexicon of the New Testament and Other Early Christian Literature.* Ed. Frederick W. Danker. Chicago: University of Chicago Press, 2000.

Brown, Driver and Briggs, *The Brown-Driver-Briggs Hebrew and English Lexicon.* Peabody, MA: Hendrickson Publishers, Inc, 2003.

Caprara, Giovanni, Ed. *The Solar System*, First Ed. Buffalo, NY: Firefly Books, 2003.

Cox, Brian and Forshaw, Jeff. *Why does E-mc²?* Cambridge, MA: Da Capo Press, 2009.

Darwin, Charles. *On the Origin of the Species by Means of Natural Selection; Or, the Preservation of Favored Races in the Struggle of Life.* Reprint. Rockville, MD: Wildside Press, 2003.

Davies, Paul. *Cosmic Jackpot: Why our Universe is Just Right for Life*. New York: Houghton Mifflin Company, 2007.

Erickson, Jon. *Historical Geology*. New York: Facts On File, 2002.

Hawking, Stephen. *A Brief History of Time*. New York: Bantam Books, 1998.

Krauss, Lawrence. *A Universe From Nothing*. New York: Free Press, 2012.

Luther, Martin. *Luther's Large Catechism,* Ed. Rodney L. Rathman. St. Louis, MO: Concordia Publishing House, 2010.

Luther, Martin. *Vol. 1: Luther's works: Genesis 1-5,* Ed. J. J. Pelikan. St. Louis, MO: Concordia Publishing House, 1958.

Luther, Martin. *Vol. 3: Luther's works, Lectures on Genesis: Chapters 15–20,* Ed. J. J. Pelikan, H. C. Oswald, and H. T. Lehmann. Saint Louis, MO: Concordia Publishing House, 1999.

Luther, Martin. *Vol. 54: Luther's works: Table Talk,* Ed. J. J. Pelikan, H. C. Oswald, and H. T. Lehmann. Philadelphia: Fortress Press, 1999.

Mathews, K. A. *Vol. 1A: Genesis 1–11:26, The New American Commentary*. Nashville: Broadman and Holman Publishers, 1996.

Oakley, Francis. *The Medieval Experience*. Toronto: University of Toronto Press, 1997.

Rees, Martin. *From Here to Infinity: A Vision for the Future of Science*. New York: W. W. Norton and Co., Inc., 2012.

Wingren, Gustav. *Man and the Incarnation,* Trans. Ross Mackenzie. Eugene, OR: Wipf and Stock Publishers, 2004.

ENDNOTES

1. Charles Darwin, *On the Origin of the Species by Means of Natural Selection; Or, the Preservation of Favored Races in the Struggle of Life,* Reprint (Rockville, MD: Wildside Press, 2003), 1.
2. Darwin, 488.
3. Francis Oakley, *The Medieval Experience* (Toronto: Universtiy of Toronto Press, 1997), 113.
4. "But as for you, continue in what you have learned and have firmly believed, knowing from whom you learned it and how from childhood you have been acquainted with the sacred writings, which are able to make you wise for salvation through faith in Christ Jesus. All Scripture is breathed out by God and profitable for teaching, for reproof, for correction, and for training in righteousness" (2 Timothy 3:14–16).
5. "All Scripture is breathed out by God and profitable for teaching, for reproof, for correction, and for training in righteousness" (2 Timothy 3:16).
6. "Now to him who is able to strengthen you according to my gospel and the preaching of Jesus Christ, according to the revelation of the mystery that was kept secret for long ages but has now been disclosed and through the prophetic writings has been made known to all nations,

according to the command of the eternal God, to bring about the obedience of faith—to the only wise God be glory forevermore through Jesus Christ! Amen" (Romans 16:25–27). "He has blessed us in the Beloved. In him we have redemption through his blood, the forgiveness of our trespasses, according to the riches of his grace, which he lavished upon us, in all wisdom and insight making known to us the mystery of his will, according to his purpose, which he set forth in Christ as a plan for the fullness of time, to unite all things in him, things in heaven and things on Earth" (Ephesians 1:6–10). "I became a minister according to the stewardship from God that was given to me for you, to make the word of God fully known, the mystery hidden for ages and generations but now revealed to his saints. To them God chose to make known how great among the Gentiles are the riches of the glory of this mystery, which is Christ in you, the hope of glory" (Colossians 1:25–27). "Great indeed, we confess, is the mystery of godliness: He was manifested in the flesh, vindicated by the Spirit, seen by angels, proclaimed among the nations, believed on in the world, taken up in glory" (1 Timothy 3:16).

7.   M. Luther, *Vol. 54: Luther's works, Table Talk*, Ed. J. J. Pelikan, H. C. Oswald, and H. T. Lehmann (Philadelphia: Fortress Press, 1999), 359.

8.   Darwin, 488.

9.   Martin Luther, *Luther's Large Catechism*, Ed. Rodney L. Rathmann (St. Louis, MO: Concordia Publishing House, 2010), 18.

10. Dylan Lovan, "Bill Nye: Creationism Threatens U.S. Science," *Associated Press*, September, 24 2012, accessed online December 7, 2012, http://www.huffingtonpost.com/2012/09/24/bill-nye-creationism-science_n_1908926.html.

11. Martin Rees, *From Here to Infinity: A Vision for the Future of Science* (New York: W. W. Norton and Co., Inc., 2012), 9.
12. Darwin, 488.
13. Darwin, 394.
14. Darwin, 450.
15. Darwin, 196.
16. Darwin, 456.
17. Darwin, 282.
18. Darwin, 490.
19. Darwin, 484.
20. Darwin, 469–470.
21. Stephen Hawking, *A Brief History of Time* (New York: Bantam Books, 1998), 21.
22. Hawking, 35.
23. Lawrence Krauss, *A Universe From Nothing* (New York: Free Press, 2012), 18.
24. Hawking, 43.
25. Krauss, 43.
26. Krauss, 46.
27. Krauss, 153.
28. Krause, 156.
29. Krauss, 3.
30. Krauss, 17.
31. Krauss, 19.
32. B. W. Eakins and G. F. Sharman, *Volumes of the World's Oceans from ETOPO1 (Boulder, CO:* NOAA National Geophysical Data Center, 2010).
33. The evangelist, St. John, expressed this sentiment towards the end of his gospel when he commented on what Jesus was able to accomplish in his earthly life. "Now there are also many other things that Jesus did. Were every one of them to be written, I suppose that the world itself could not contain the books that would be written" (John 21:25). If

this is true of the work of Jesus during his earthly ministry, which we know was just a few short years, how much more so when considering the eternal depth of Elohim?

34. F. Brown, S. Driver and C. Briggs, *The Brown-Driver-Briggs Hebrew and English Lexicon* (Peabody, MA: Hendrickson Publishers, Inc, 2003), 1062.

35. Brown, 96.

36. Brown, 365.

37. The claims that the Bible makes regarding the key events in salvation history, such as creation and the bodily resurrection of Christ are so important that St. Paul belabors this point in a letter written to the churches of Corinth. "Now if Christ is proclaimed as raised from the dead, how can some of you say that there is no resurrection of the dead? But if there is no resurrection of the dead, then not even Christ has been raised. And if Christ has not been raised, then our preaching is in vain and your faith is in vain. We are even found to be misrepresenting God, because we testified about God that he raised Christ, whom he did not raise if it is true that the dead are not raised. For if the dead are not raised, not even Christ has been raised. And *if Christ has not been raised, your faith is futile* and you are still in your sins. Then those also who have fallen asleep in Christ have perished. *If in Christ we have hope in this life only, we are of all people most to be pitied*" (1 Corinthians 15:12–19, emphasis added). Apparently, some in Corinth thought they were doing the faith some service by placating their pagan audience and adapting the message to fit the sensibilities of their contemporaries. If a person must be careful handling a sharp knife so that he or she doesn't accidentally cut himself or herself, how much more so for those who are handling the very Word of God in the Scriptures?

38. Hawking, 121.

39. Krause, 15.

40. Hawking, 44.

41. "WMAP Produces New Results," National Atmospheric and Space Administration, accessed January 22, 2013, http://map.gsfc.nasa.gov/news/index.html.

42. "WMAP Produces New Results."

43. "WMAP Produces New Results."

44. Brown, 956.

45. "Planetary Fact Sheet—US units," National Atmospheric and Space Administration, accessed December 13, 2012, http://nssdc.gsfc.nasa.gov/planetary/factsheet/planet_table_british.html.

46. "Comet Halley Summary," Jet Propulsion Laboratory Office of Public Information, accessed December 13, 2012, http://er.jsc.nasa.gov/seh/halley.html.

47. "Comet Hale-Bopp," National Atmospheric and Space Administration, accessed December 13, 2012, http://nssdc.gsfc.nasa.gov/planetary/halebopp.html.

48. Joel Achenbach, "Alpha Centauri May Have Habitable Planets, if Only We Can Get There," *Washington Post,* June 1, 2009, accessed September 11, 2012, http://www.washingtonpost.com/wp-dyn/content/article/2009/05/31/AR2009053102082.html.

49. Krauss, 141–142.

50. Krauss, 111

51. *Webster's New College Dictionary II, 3rd Ed.* (New York: Houghton-Mifflin, 2008), 1182.

52. M. Luther, *Vol. 1: Luther's works: Genesis 1-5,* Ed. J. J. Pelikan (St. Louis, MO: Concordia Publishing House, 1958), 11.

53. "Faster Than Light Particles May Be Physics Revolution," Reuters, accessed October 5, 2012, http://www.foxnews.com/scitech/2011/09/23/faster-than-light-particles-may-be-physics-revolution/.

54. Darwin, 120–121.

55. Eugene C. Robertson, "The Interior of the Earth," United States Geological Society, accessed September 25, 2012, http://pubs.usgs.gov/gip/interior/.

56. W. E. Holt and T. C. Wallace, "Crustal thickness and upper mantle velocities in the Tibetan Plateau Region from the inversion of regional Pnl waveforms: Evidence for a thick upper mantle lid beneath southern Tibet," *Journal of Geophysical Research,* 95 (1990): B8, accessed September 25, 2012, doi:10.1029/JB095iB08p12499.

57. Robertson.

58. Ebubekir Altunas and Sekeroglu, Ahmet, "Mechanical Behavior and Physical Properties of Chicken Egg as Affected by Different Egg Weights," *Journal of Food Process Engineering,* 33 (2010): 1, accessed September 25, 2012 doi:10.1111/j.1745-4530.2008.00263.x.

59. Krauss, xv.

60. Jon Erickson, *Historical Geology* (New York: Facts On File, 2002), 17.

61. Erickson, 24–27.

62. Erickson, 35.

63. "It's the Little Things that Matter," NASA Earth Observatory, accessed October 22, 2012, http://Earthobservatory.nasa.gov/Features/OceanProductivity/page2.php.

64. Darwin, 490.

65. Darwin, 488.

66. Harald Furnes, et. al. "Early Life Recorded in Archean Pillow Lavas" *Science* 304 (2004): 578, accessed October 24, 2012 doi 10.1126/science.1095858. This article discusses the significance of tubes bored by early microbes into rock that has been estimated at 3.5 billion years old. If the earth is believed to be 4.5–4.6 billion years old, then this is evidence of life very early in the earth's history. The dates

don't match well with Moses, but the evidence of early life most certainly does.

67. Darwin, 313–316.
68. Hawking, 38.
69. Krauss, 33.
70. Giovanni Caprara, Ed., *The Solar System* (Buffalo, NY: Firefly Books, 2003), 51.
71. Caprara, 17–21.
72. Erickson, 3, 6.
73. Erickson, 3.
74. P. H. Roberts and G. A. Glatzmaier, "Geodynamo Theory and Simulations," *Reviews of Modern Physics,* 72 (October 2000): 1081.
75. Caprara, 29, 46.
76. Richard Thompson, "Power Failure in Canada in 1989," Australian Government Bureau of Meteorology Radio and Space Weather Services, accessed October 11, 2012, http://www.ips.gov.au/Educational/1/3/12.
77. Roberts and Glatzmaier, 1087. For brevity's sake, the following paragraph well summarizes their conclusions most applicable for this discussion: "The Temperature *T* beneath the crust exceeds the Curie point of all known materials; permanent magnetism does not exist anywhere in the Earth, except the crust. The obvious explanation of the Earth's magnetism is therefore untenable; the main field is created by electric currents flowing mainly in the core.[6] Several possible origins of these currents have been proposed,[7] but all except one have been found wanting. The favored idea today is that they are generated by self-excited dynamo action associated with the motion of core fluid, a suggestion first made by Larmor (1919)."
78. Roberts and Glatzmaier, 1085.
79. Caprera, 109–110.
80. Caprera, 110.

81. Caprera, 100.

82. K. A. Mathews, *Vol. 1A: Genesis 1–11:26, The New American Commentary* (Nashville: Broadman and Holman Publishers, 1996), 154.

83. Krauss, 17, 19, 96–97, 99, 104, 113, 126.

84. Deuteronomy 34.

85. "Hear, O Israel: The LORD our God, the LORD is one. You shall love the LORD your God with all your heart and with all your soul and with all your might" (Deuteronomy 6:4–5).

86. Brown, 1056. Literally "swarmers" or "swarming things." Refers to creatures that have a habit of congregating. Mice, rats, birds, and schooling fish can all be included under this term depending on the context. In this verse, it denotes any such creature that dwells in the seas or skies.

87. Camilo Mora et al. "How Many Species Are There on Earth and in the Ocean?" PLOS Biology 9 (2011): 8, doi:10.1371/journal.pbio.1001127. 2011. 5.

88. J. B. S. Haldane, *What is Life?* (London: Lindsay Drummond, 1949), 258.

89. "Volumes of the World's Oceans from ETOPO1," NOAA National Geophysical Data Center, accessed December 24, 2012, http://ngdc.noaa.gov/mgg/global/etopo1_ocean_volumes.html.

90. Philippe Bouchet, *The Exploration of Marine Biodiversity: Scientific and Technological Challenges* (Madrid, Spain: Fundación BBVA, 2006), 50.

91. Bouchet, 54.

92. Erickson, 33.

93. Paul Davies, *Cosmic Jackpot: Why our Universe is Just Right for Life* (New York: Houghton Mifflin, 2007), 264.

94. Darwin, 95–96.

95. Bouchet, 38.

96. Darwin, 51.

97. M. Luther, *Luther's works, vol. 1: Lectures on Genesis: Chapters 1–5*, Ed. J. J. Pelikan, H. C. Oswald, and H. T. Lehmann (Saint Louis, MO: Concordia Publishing House, 1958), 62.

98. The psalmist wrote, "Yet you have made him a little lower than the heavenly beings and crowned him with glory and honor. You have given him dominion over the works of your hands; you have put all things under his feet" (Psalm 8:5–6). By giving Adam dominion over the works of His hands, Elohim has lifted up and exalted humanity. Not even the angels are said to have any power and authority in and of themselves. Elohim gave such to human beings, who were created in His image.

99. Gustav Wingren, *Man and the Incarnation*, Trans. Ross Mackenzie (Eugene, OR: Wipf and Stock Publishers, 2004), 26.

100. Iwasaki, Kenji, et al. *Health Problems due to Long Working Hours in Japan: Working Hours, Workers' Compensation (Karoshi), and Preventive Measures* (Industrial Health, 2006), 538-539.

101. Wingren, 26.

102. William Waldron, "Common Ground, Common Cause: Buddhism and Science on the Afflictions of Self-Identity," accessed December 20, 2012, http://www.gampoabbey.org/documents/Waldron-CommonGround.pdf.

103. Davies, 222–223.

104. Krauss, 159.

105. "Share in suffering for the gospel by the power of God, who saved us and called us to a holy calling, not because of our works but because of his own purpose and grace, which he gave us in Christ Jesus before the ages began, and which now has been manifested through the appearing of our Savior Christ Jesus, who abolished death and brought life and immortality to light through the gospel" (2 Timothy 1:8–10).

106. Martin Luther, *Luther's works, vol. 3: Lectures on Genesis: Chapters 15–20*, Ed. J. J. Pelikan, H. C. Oswald, and H. T. Lehmann (Saint Louis, MO: Concordia Publishing House, 1999), Genesis 17:11, electronic edition.

107. Romans 5:12–21.

108. In Genesis 5, Moses implicitly stated that humanity no longer had the image of God. In the genealogy account, he carefully reiterated that Adam was created in God's image but then contrasted the image Seth inherited from Adam to the image of God, in which Adam was created. "This is the book of the generations of Adam. *When God created man, he made him in the likeness of God*. Male and female he created them, and he blessed them and named them Man when they were created. When Adam had lived 130 years, he fathered a son *in his own likeness, after his image,* and named him Seth" (Genesis 5:1–3, emphasis added).

CPSIA information can be obtained at www.ICGtesting.com
Printed in the USA
LVOW13s1212290713

345138LV00002B/4/P